MOON

– BEST OF –

# ZION & BRYCE

T0036027

Maya Silver

# ZION & BRYCE CANYON NATIONAL PARKS

To Salt Lake City

Cedar City Regional Airport

15

Cedar City

14

Brian Head

North View

Hamiltons Fort

Lake Quichapa

Ashdown Gorge Wilderness

Cedar Breaks National Monument

Dixie National Forest

Spring Creek Canyon Wilderness Study Area

Kanarraville

Navajo Lake

KOLOB CANYONS VISITOR CENTER

Deep Creek North Wilderness Area

15

KOLOB CANYONS VIEWPOINT

KOLOB CANYONS

To St. George and Las Vegas

Red Butte Wilderness Area

Upper Kolob Plateau

Horse Pasture Plateau

Deep Creek Wilderness Area

North Fork Virgin River

The Narrows

Blackridge Wilderness Area

Lower Kolob Plateau

Zion National Park

THE NARROWS

Hurricane Mesa

EMERALD POOLS TRAILS

ZION CANYON

EAST ENTRANCE

ZION-MOUNT CARMEL HWY

9

Mount Carmel Junction

ZION-MOUNT CARMEL HIGHWAY

SOUTH ENTRANCE

9

Virgin

ZION CANYON VISITOR CENTER

Springdale

Virgin River

Grafton (ghost town)

Rockville

East Fork Virgin River

Parunuweap Canyon Wilderness Study Area

Apple Valley

Canaan Mountain Wilderness Area

© MOON.COM

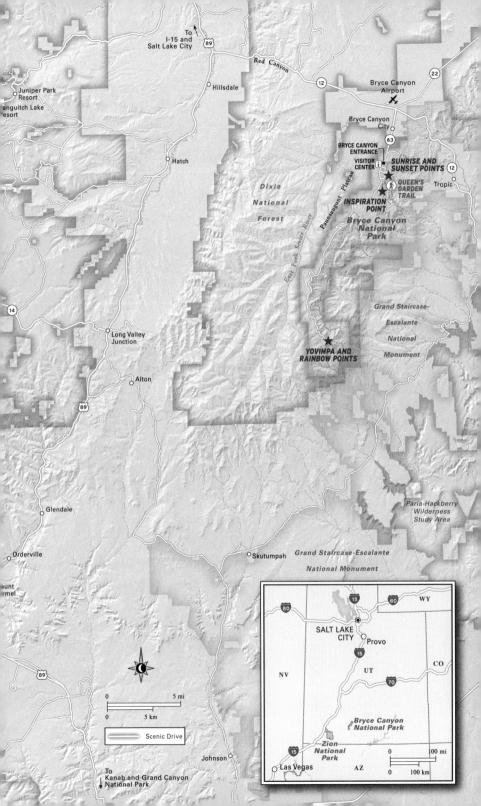

# CONTENTS

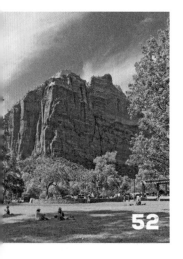

90

116

126

Zion Canyon

# WELCOME TO
# ZION & BRYCE

Awe and adventure await in southern Utah.

Zion National Park is all about stunning contrasts, with towering canyon walls soaring above an oasis of cottonwood trees and wildflowers along the Virgin River. Bryce Canyon National Park is famed for its sandstone spires—called hoodoos—huddled along a steep mountainside. At sunrise or sunset, the trails empty and the hoodoos glow.

There are countless ways to explore the parks. Trek through narrow canyons, take a scenic drive past extraordinary vistas, or get up close with hoodoos on horseback. Whatever you choose, once you've experienced this beautiful red rock landscape, you'll want to come back for more.

Riverside Walk in Zion Canyon

# BEST DAY IN
# ZION & BRYCE

# 𝓜orning

**1** Get an early start and make your first stop the **Zion Canyon Visitor Center,** where you can fill up your water bottles, then board the Zion Canyon shuttle (page 74).

**2** Hop off at Zion Lodge and warm up with the easy hike to **Lower Emerald Pool** (page 62).

**3** Ride to the end of the shuttle route and exit at Temple of Sinawava, where you can catch the paved **Riverside Walk** (2 mi/3.2 km round-trip) along the Virgin River. Check out the hanging gardens—plants growing from cracks in the cliff walls. At the walk's end, the trail goes into the river. Wade in as far as you're comfortable—it's a great way to cool off on a hot Zion day. Hiking the full Narrows requires specialized gear, so save that for a future trip (page 64).

**4** Ride the shuttle back to **Zion Lodge** and grab a quick lunch at the Castle Dome Café before returning to the visitor center and your car (page 71).

# *Afternoon*

**5** Make the drive to Bryce a scenic one. From Zion Canyon, **Zion-Mount Carmel Highway** leads up a series of switchbacks to East Zion's high plateau. Highlights worth stopping for include the Great Arch of Zion, Checkerboard Mesa, and the 1-mile (1.6-km) round-trip Canyon Overlook Trail (page 55).

**6** Once in Bryce, head down **Queen's Garden Trail** from Sunrise Point to commune with the hoodoos (page 98).

7 Follow the scenic drive up to its apex at **Yovimpa and Rainbow Points** for the perfect panorama (page 94).

# Evening

**8** It's time for a real meal—enjoy dinner at the **Lodge at Bryce Canyon** (page 106).

**9** Afterward, a stroll on the **Rim Trail** between Sunset and Sunrise Points beholds spires that glow orange and pink as the sun goes down (page 95).

**10** If you're up for it, join the flock of photographers at **Sunset Point** to catch the sunset. Bryce is just as spectacular after dark—the absence of light pollution makes it an excellent place to view the Milky Way (page 90).

## ITINERARY DETAILS

- This itinerary works best **April–October.**
- Avoid the largest crowds and intense heat by traveling **outside the July–August window.**
- Make **reservations** for **lodging and dining** up to a year in advance at Zion Lodge (888/297-2757; www.zionlodge.com) or at the Lodge at Bryce Canyon (877/386-4383; www.visitbrycecanyon.com); however, last-minute bookings may be available. The Lodge at Bryce Canyon is open April–October.
- Check to make sure **shuttle reservations** aren't required at Zion—rules may shift as the National Park Service works to keep up with the crowds.
- Stuff your pack with a **picnic lunch,** more **water** than you think you need, **sunscreen,** and **snacks.**
- **Parking** may be full, especially in summer, at Zion. Pay for parking in Springdale for easy access to the free Zion-Springdale shuttle.

hoodoos along Navajo Loop Trail

# SEASONS OF ZION & BRYCE

The moderate temperatures of **spring** and **early fall** make these seasons generally the best for a visit, though both parks are open year-round. April through October is the busiest time of year, when popular campgrounds and hotels may be booked out well in advance.

## SPRING
### (LATE MAR.-EARLY JUNE)
In early spring, Zion Canyon is pleasant, while Bryce—at elevations ranging 6,600-9,100 feet (2,012-2,774 m)—can be snowy well into the season. That also means that come summer, Bryce is more pleasant than Zion and much of southern Utah.

### Temperatures
**Day:** 54-73°F (12 to 23°C)
**Night:** 29-43°F (-2 to 6°C)

## Road and Trail Conditions
Snowmelt and spring showers may result in wet trails, particularly around Bryce's higher elevations and on shaded trails. Early spring storms can also wreak havoc on backcountry roads. Whether you're hiking or driving, turn back if you encounter muddy conditions to avoid damaging trails or getting hopelessly stuck.

## SUMMER
### (LATE JUNE-EARLY SEPT.)
Thunderstorms are fairly common in summer and bring the threat of flash flooding, especially in slot canyons. By July-August, it's downright hot in Zion, while July is the warmest month in Bryce.

### Temperatures
**Day:** 80-100°F (27 to 38°C)
**Night:** 57-68°F (14 to 20°C)

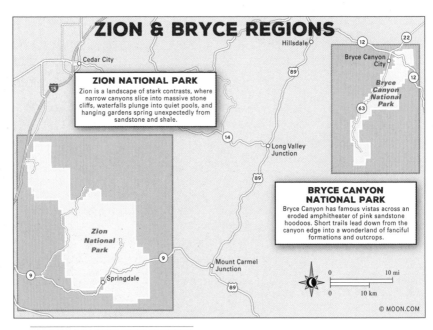

ZION & BRYCE REGIONS

Hillsdale

Cedar City

**ZION NATIONAL PARK**
Zion is a landscape of stark contrasts, where narrow canyons slice into massive stone cliffs, waterfalls plunge into quiet pools, and hanging gardens spring unexpectedly from sandstone and shale.

Bryce Canyon City

Bryce Canyon National Park

Long Valley Junction

Zion National Park

**BRYCE CANYON NATIONAL PARK**
Bryce Canyon has famous vistas across an eroded amphitheater of pink sandstone hoodoos. Short trails lead down from the canyon edge into a wonderland of fanciful formations and outcrops.

Springdale

Mount Carmel Junction

0        10 mi
0     10 km

© MOON.COM

Bryce Canyon in winter

visitors should pack warm clothing and not be shocked to encounter snow.

## Temperatures
**Day:** 57-78°F (14 to 26°C)
**Night:** 27-49°F (-3 to 9°C)

## Road and Trail Conditions
In early fall, road and trail conditions are usually similar to what you'd encounter in summer. Later in October, snow may start to fall, turning dirt into mud and potentially creating snowy conditions at higher elevations in Bryce.

## Road and Trail Conditions
Trails and dirt roads are usually dry and in good condition throughout summer. The exception is when thunderstorms loom, bringing the threat of flash floods that can suddenly inundate trails or roads that pass through narrow canyons. Keep tabs on the forecast to avoid getting yourself in a serious pickle. The only other undesirable condition you may encounter is dust, resulting from extended dry periods.

## EARLY FALL
### (SEPT.-OCT.)
September and October are lovely times to visit Zion, with moderate temperatures during the day and cool nights. Pack layers, because temperatures can easily vary by 30 degrees Fahrenheit (17 degrees C) from sunrise to midday. Late October is a good time to see Zion decked out in fall foliage. Since Bryce is at a considerably higher elevation, October

## LATE FALL-WINTER
### (NOV.-EARLY MAR.)
Red rock looks especially enchanting after snowfall. Winter can be a great time to visit the high country around Bryce, where cross-country skiers take to the park roads. It's also the least crowded time to explore Zion, if you don't mind bundling up.

## Temperatures
**Day:** 36-48°F (2 to 9°C)
**Night:** 12-24°F (-11 to -4°C)

## Road and Trail Conditions
The roads within and around Zion are usually fine, except during the chance snowstorm. A few thousand feet higher in elevation at Bryce, the roads are riskier come winter. While these roads are plowed, during or following a storm, sections of Bryce's main scenic drive may be closed, so 4WD vehicles and snow tires are recommended. A few highways in the Zion-Bryce area do close for the winter, most notably those around Cedar Breaks National Monument.

Rainbow Point

# BEST OF THE BEST
# ZION & BRYCE

# BEST HIKES

## ZION
### Emerald Pools Trails
**MODERATE**

Starting from The Grotto, hike **Kayenta Trail** to access the **Upper, Middle, and Lower Emerald Pools Trails** to ponds, spectacular waterfalls, and hanging gardens (page 62).

### West Rim Trail to Angels Landing
**STRENUOUS; PERMIT REQUIRED**

Climb steadily rising West Rim Trail through a series of switchbacks to Scout Lookout, then grab hold of a chain to traverse the final stretch to a 360-degree view of the canyon at Angels Landing. This is not a hike for kids (page 58).

### The Narrows
**STRENUOUS**

It's hard to say what's better—hiking through the Virgin River on a hot day or peering up at 2,000-foot-tall (610-m) sandstone walls that narrow upstream into a slot canyon. Technical footwear and trekking poles (available to rent in Springdale) are strongly recommended (page 64).

## BRYCE
### Queen's Garden Trail
**EASY-MODERATE**

This popular trail drops from Sunrise Point through impressive features in the middle of Bryce Amphitheater to a hoodoo resembling a portly Queen Victoria. Queen's Garden also makes

---

## NEED TO KNOW: ZION

- **Park website:** www.nps.gov/zion
- **Entrance fee:** $35 per vehicle
- **Main entrance:** South Entrance
- **Main visitor venter:** Zion Canyon Visitor Center
- **Hotel and park activity reservations:** www.zionlodge.com
- **Campsite reservations:** www.recreation.gov
- **Permits:** Permits (cost varies by permit type; www.zionpermits.nps.gov) are required for popular hikes like Angels Landing, canyoneering routes, and overnight trips in the park.
- **Gas in the park:** None available inside the park. Gas up in Springdale, just south of the main entrance.
- **High season:** Apr.-Sept.

Angels Landing (left); Queen's Garden Trail (right)

a good loop with Navajo Loop and Rim Trails (page 98).

### Navajo Loop Trail
**MODERATE**

From Sunset Point along the rim, descend past sweeping views of Bryce Amphitheater into a hoodoo-filled basin. Navajo Loop leads into narrow Wall Street Canyon and connects with other trails for a longer hike (page 97).

## NEED TO KNOW: BRYCE

- **Park website:** www.nps.gov/brca
- **Entrance fee:** $35 per vehicle
- **Main entrance:** Hwy. 63 (north side of Bryce Canyon National Park)
- **Main visitor center:** Bryce Canyon Visitor Center
- **Hotel and park activity reservations:** www.visitbrycecanyon.com
- **Campsite reservations:** www.recreation.gov
- **Permits:** Permits ($10, plus $5 per person; www.recreation.gov) are required for overnight backpacking trips in the park.
- **Gas in the park:** None available inside park. Gas up at Ruby's Inn, just north of the Bryce Canyon entrance.
- **High season:** May-Sept.

hoodoos in Bryce Canyon National Park

# BEST VIEWS

## ZION
### Court of the Patriarchs Viewpoint
For an eyeful without a hike, jump off the shuttle bus at the Court of the Patriarchs (page 51).

### Angels Landing
You'll work for it, but Angels Landing beholds what's unequivocally considered the best view in Zion. An early park visitor inspired the name with his observation that only angels could land upon a peak so high (page 58).

## BRYCE
### Sunrise Point
The name may be cliché, but the angle of the rising sun really does make this viewpoint in Bryce spectacular. Its nearby counterpart, Sunset Point, is equally lovely (page 90).

### Inspiration Point
This cluster of three viewpoints beholds row upon row of hoodoos lining the amphitheater below. Climb a short but steep path to the highest point for a heavy dose of awe (page 90).

### Yovimpa and Rainbow Points
At the park's highest point (9,100 ft/2,773 m), you can see the cliffs of the Grand Staircase. Bryce's formations were sculpted from the Pink Cliffs, below which you can see the Gray and White Cliffs, plus a Vermillion Cliff layer at the bottom (page 94).

Court of the Patriarchs Viewpoint

# ROAD STOPS BETWEEN ZION & BRYCE

Red Canyon

The trip from Zion's main entrance to Bryce is 84 miles (135 km)—a little under two hours' drive along U.S. 89. It's just long enough that you might want some diversions along the way. If you're starting in Bryce and heading to Zion, reverse the order.

- **Rock Shops:** There are lots of rocks in the hills—get a bagful the easy way at **The Rock Stop** (385 W. State St., Orderville; 435/648-2747). The friendly owners also make a great cup of coffee.

- **Diner Fare:** Family-run since 1931, **Thunderbird Restaurant** (4530 State St., Mount Carmel; 435/648-2262; www.thunderbirdutah.com; Tues.-Sun.) serves up homemade pie and retro Western memorabilia amid its cozy booths.

- **Zip Line:** Soar on two zip lines (one that accommodates an adult and a small child) at **Mystic River Outdoor Adventures** (5000 U.S. 89; 435/648-2823; http://mysticriveradventures.com). This small family-run park north of Glendale also has a fishing pond.

- **Horseback Rides:** Even if you're not spending the night, pull off at the **Bryce Zion Campground** (5 mi/8.1 km north of Glendale; 435/648-2823; https://brycezioncampground.net) and saddle up for a guided trail ride. The campground makes a good base for visiting both national parks.

- **Red Canyon:** Pause and take a breath before you get to busy Bryce. Red Canyon has lots of hiking and biking trails among its sandstone spires.

Angels Landing

# BEST SCENIC DRIVE

## ZION-MOUNT CARMEL HIGHWAY

**DRIVING DISTANCE:** 24.5 miles (39.4 km) one-way
**DRIVING TIME:** 2 hours one-way
**START:** Zion Canyon Visitor Center
**END:** Mount Carmel Junction

From Zion Canyon, this road climbs through a series of switchbacks and passes through a crazy long tunnel (as well as a much shorter one). This drive provides access to the canyons and high plateaus east of Zion Canyon, where you'll find fewer hikers than on the canyon trails. Take the easy 1-mile (1.6-km) round-trip **Canyon Overlook Trail** to peer down at the massive **Great Arch of Zion,** a "blind" arch that's not carved all the way through. Even if you're not up for a hike, stop at **Checkerboard Mesa,** a massive hill of hatch-marked sandstone right off the road. From the east entrance to the park, the road continues about 13 miles (20.9 km) to its junction with U.S. 89. From here, head north to Bryce Canyon National Park (page 55).

Checkerboard Mesa

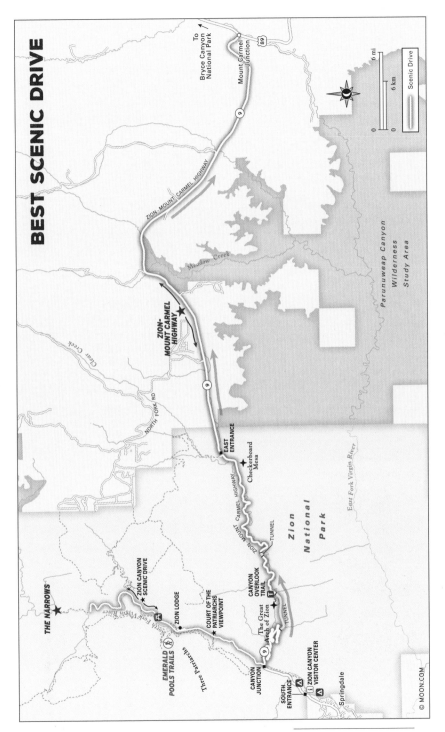

BEST SCENIC DRIVE

# INDIGENOUS PEOPLES OF ZION & BRYCE

Indigenous people have lived in Utah for thousands of years, including in present-day Zion National Park, where an **Ancestral Puebloan** settlement has been found. Thousands of stone dwellings, ceremonial kivas, and towers still stand today in Utah.

About 800 years ago, the Ancestral Puebloans departed from the region, as did a people known today as the Fremont. Their reasons for leaving? Possibly a megadrought, warfare, disease, or a combination of the three, though this exodus is a mystery still being unearthed by archaeologists. Some Ancestral Puebloans moved south and joined the Pueblo people of present-day Arizona and New Mexico.

When the Latter-day Saints arrived in the 1840s, Native Americans resided in the river canyons. Federal reservations were granted to five major tribes, though dozens more live in the area as well. Today, approximately 60,000 Indigenous people call Utah home.

## UTE

Several bands of Utes (Núuci) ranged over large areas of what is now central and eastern Utah and adjacent Colorado. Originally hunter-gatherers, they acquired horses around 1800. Customs adopted from Plains people included the use of rawhide, tepees, and the travois, a sled used to carry goods. The discovery of gold in southern Colorado and the pressures of farmers there and in Utah forced the Utes to move and renegotiate treaties again and again. Current Ute reservations include the Uintah and Ouray Indian Reservation in northeast Utah, the small White Mesa Indian Reservation in southeast

Ancient Native Americans left behind an incredible rock art legacy in Utah.

Utah, and the Ute Mountain Indian Reservation in southwest Colorado and northwest New Mexico.

## SOUTHERN PAIUTE

Six of the 19 major bands of Southern Paiutes (Nuwuvi) lived along the Santa Clara, Beaver, and Virgin Rivers, as well as in other parts of southwest Utah. Historically, extended families hunted and gathered food together. Fishing and the cultivation of corn, beans, squash, and sunflowers supplemented the diet of most of the communities. Today, Utah's Paiutes are headquartered in Cedar City and across scattered parcels of reservation land. Southern Paiutes also live in southern Nevada and northern Arizona.

## NAVAJO

Also known as the Diné (meaning "the people"), the Navajo moved into the San Juan River area around 1600. Many Navajo crafts and religious practices were influenced by other Native Americans and Spanish settlers. The Navajo were the first in the area to move away from hunting and gathering, transitioning to the farming and shepherding techniques they learned from the Spanish. The Navajo are one of the largest Native American groups in the country, with 16 million acres of exceptionally scenic land in southeast Utah and adjacent Arizona and New Mexico. The Navajo Nation's headquarters is at Window Rock, Arizona.

## SIGHTS

The **Zion Human History Museum** displays Ancestral Puebloan artifacts. As you explore **Bryce,** keep in mind that early indigenous peoples considered some hoodoo areas to be sacred spaces.

Zion Human History Museum

# BEST GEOLOGIC FEATURES

## ZION

### Three Patriarchs

Three towering sandstone peaks—named by a Methodist minister for Old Testament patriarchs Abraham, Isaac, and Jacob—are best photographed when morning sunlight highlights their orange, pink, and white tones (page 51).

### Great White Throne

This 2,350-foot (716-m) mountain is composed of mostly white Navajo sandstone. It's visible from many points in the canyon, but the best views are from the Big Bend shuttle stop (page 55).

## BRYCE

### "Silent City"

Inspiration Point gives a good view of this dense concentration of hoodoos and sandstone fins rising from the canyon floor. Whether the city is full of tall buildings or people standing shoulder to shoulder is up to your imagination (page 90).

Three Patriarchs

# TRAVEL SUSTAINABLY IN ZION & BRYCE

Zion shuttle

Bryce Canyon and Zion National Parks are actively involved with reducing the parks' carbon footprint and encouraging sustainability through a variety of initiatives. For example, both parks operate fleets of electric, battery hybrid, and alternative fuel vehicles for transportation, maintenance, enforcement, and administrative purposes. In addition, both parks use specially shielded lights to minimize light pollution and reduce the impact of artificial light on nocturnal creatures. Here's how you can help:

- Rather than driving, bike or use the **shuttles** offered in both parks during high season. (In Zion, the road closes to private vehicles during high season, so use of the shuttle is currently required.)

- Zion and Bryce also provide **recycling containers** in all guest rooms and public areas. Use them. Better yet, bring a **refillable water bottle,** as both parks have established water refill stations to reduce the use of single-use plastic water bottles.

- **Stay on marked trails,** and respect signage indicating areas that are off limits. This will help keep you safe and preserve the trail and its surrounding environment. Creating unofficial trails or shortcuts can harm delicate plant life and erode soil.

Angels Landing

# ZION NATIONAL PARK

With its sheer cliffs and monoliths reaching into the sky, Zion is magic. Energetic streams and other forces of erosion created this land of finely sculptured rock. Water percolating through massive chunks of sandstone over millennia has carved both dramatic canyons and an incredible variety of niche ecosystems.

The canyon's name is credited to Isaac Behunin, a Latter-day Saint who observed that the area lent itself to spiritual worship. When Brigham Young visited later, however, he found tobacco and wine in use and declared the place "not Zion"—which some dutiful followers began calling it.

Zion's grandeur is evident throughout the year. Spring and fall provide pleasant temperatures and the best chances of seeing wildlife and wildflowers. From mid-October through early November, cottonwoods and other trees and plants blaze with color. In winter, snow-covered slopes contrast with red rock. Snow may block some high-country trails and the road to Lava Point, but the rest of the park is open and accessible year-round.

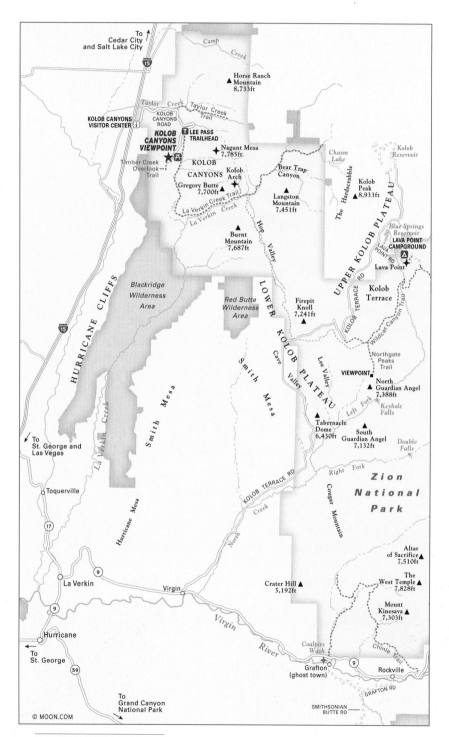

To
Cedar City
and Salt Lake City

Camp Creek

Horse Ranch
Mountain
8,733ft

Taylor Creek

Taylor Creek Trail

KOLOB CANYONS
VISITOR CENTER

KOLOB CANYONS ROAD

LEE PASS
TRAILHEAD

KOLOB CANYONS VIEWPOINT

Nagunt Mesa
7,785ft

Chasm Lake

Kolob Reservoir

Timber Creek Overlook Trail

KOLOB CANYONS

Kolob Arch

Bear Trap Canyon

The Hardscrabble

Kolob Peak
8,933ft

Gregory Butte
7,700ft

La Verkin Creek Trail

La Verkin Creek

Langston Mountain
7,451ft

UPPER KOLOB PLATEAU

Blue Springs Reservoir

LAVA POINT CAMPGROUND

Burnt Mountain
7,687ft

Hop Valley

LAVA POINT RD

Lava Point

HURRICANE CLIFFS

Blackridge Wilderness Area

Red Butte Wilderness Area

LOWER KOLOB PLATEAU

Firepit Knoll
7,241ft

Kolob Terrace

KOLOB TERRACE RD

Smith Mesa

Cave Valley

Lee Valley

Northgate Peaks Trail

Wildcat Canyon Trail

VIEWPOINT

North Guardian Angel
7,388ft

Keyhole Falls

Tabernacle Dome
6,430ft

South Guardian Angel
7,132ft

Double Falls

La Verkin Creek

Left Fork

To St. George and Las Vegas

Toquerville

Hurricane Mesa

KOLOB TERRACE RD

North Creek

Right Fork

Zion National Park

Cougar Mountain

17

La Verkin

Virgin

Crater Hill
5,192ft

Altar of Sacrifice
7,510ft

The West Temple
7,828ft

9

9

Hurricane

Virgin River

Mount Kinesava
7,303ft

To St. George

59

Coalpits Wash

Grafton (ghost town)

9

Rockville

Chinle Trail

GRAFTON RD

To Grand Canyon National Park

© MOON.COM

SMITHSONIAN BUTTE RD

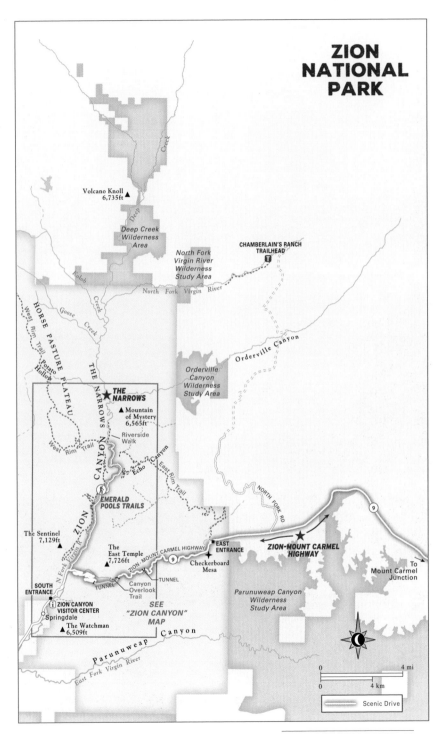

# ZION NATIONAL PARK

Volcano Knoll
6,735ft

Deep Creek
Wilderness
Area

North Fork
Virgin River
Wilderness
Study Area

CHAMBERLAIN'S RANCH
TRAILHEAD

North Fork Virgin River

Orderville Canyon

Orderville
Canyon
Wilderness
Study Area

HORSE PASTURE PLATEAU

West Rim Trail

Goose Creek

Kolob Creek

Potato Hollow

THE NARROWS

THE NARROWS

Mountain
of Mystery
6,565ft

Riverside
Walk

West Rim Trail

Echo Canyon

East Rim Trail

ZION CANYON

EMERALD
POOLS TRAILS

The Sentinel
7,129ft

The
East Temple
7,726ft

NORTH FORK RD

9

ZION-MOUNT CARMEL
HIGHWAY

N Fork Virgin R.

ZION-MOUNT CARMEL HIGHWAY

EAST
ENTRANCE

9

Checkerboard
Mesa

To
Mount Carmel
Junction

SOUTH
ENTRANCE

TUNNEL

Canyon
Overlook
Trail

TUNNEL

SEE
"ZION CANYON"
MAP

ZION CANYON
VISITOR CENTER
Springdale

The Watchman
6,509ft

Parunuweap Canyon
Wilderness
Study Area

Parunuweap Canyon

East Fork Virgin River

0        4 mi
0        4 km

Scenic Drive

# TOP 3

★ **1. ZION-MOUNT CARMEL HIGHWAY:** This 11-mile (17.7-km) drive traverses a historic tunnel and winds past some of the park's most staggering scenery (page 55).

★ **2. THE NARROWS:** Step into the Virgin River and wade upstream through canyon walls up to 2,000 feet (610 m) high (page 64).

★ **3. KOLOB CANYONS VIEWPOINT:** This overlook offers beautiful panoramas and the perfect spot to have a picnic lunch (page 72).

# ZION 3 WAYS

Zion National Park has four main sections: **Zion Canyon,** the **eastern side of Zion Canyon, Kolob Terrace,** and **Kolob Canyons.** For most visitors, the main attraction is Zion Canyon, which is approximately 2,400 feet (732 m) deep. Spring through fall, visitors are required to ride a **shuttle bus** along Zion Canyon Scenic Drive, which winds through the canyon floor—though cyclists are permitted too.

## HALF DAY

A half day is just enough time to ride the shuttle through Zion Canyon, admire the rock walls, and take a couple of easygoing hikes. An early start will gain you a spot in the visitor center parking lot, which gets crowded by 8am. It's also possible to schedule your half-day exploration in the late afternoon and early evening, as temperatures begin to drop and crowds thin. The shuttle runs until about 8pm.

**1** Browse the panels in the outdoor plaza at the **Zion Canyon Visitor Center** and get in line for the shuttle. Buses come every few minutes.

**2** While the morning light is still making the rocks glow, hop off the shuttle at the **Court of the Patriarchs Viewpoint** and take a very short trail to views of three Navajo sandstone peaks: Abraham, Isaac, and Jacob.

**3** Ride the shuttle to the Temple of Sinawava, at the end of the line. Disembark and walk the 1-mile-long (1.6-km) **Riverside Walk** trail to its end, where long-distance hikers wade into the Virgin River to traverse the Narrows.

**4** Take the shuttle back to the Zion Lodge stop. Follow the paved **Lower Emerald Pool Trail,** about 0.5 mile (0.8 km) to the pool and waterfall.

**5** Back at **Zion Lodge,** you'll have time for a quick bite at the café, or a longer sit-down meal in the lodge dining room, before returning to browse the bookstore at the visitor center and fetch your car.

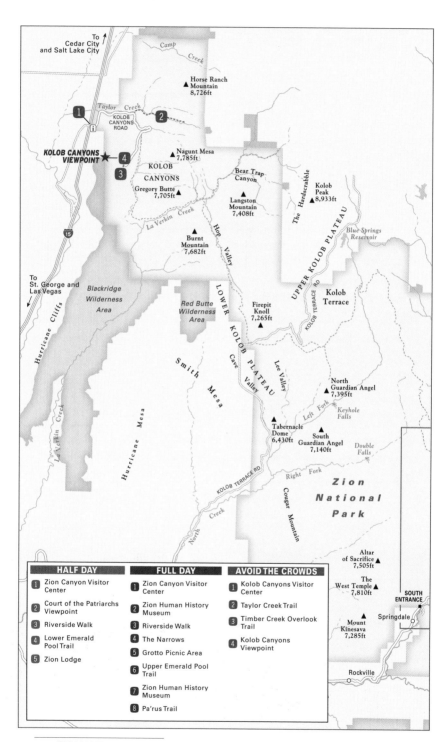

To Cedar City and Salt Lake City

Camp Creek

Horse Ranch Mountain
8,726ft

Taylor Creek

**1**  KOLOB CANYONS ROAD  **2**

**KOLOB CANYONS VIEWPOINT** ★ **4**

**3**

Nagunt Mesa
7,785ft

**KOLOB CANYONS**

Bear Trap Canyon

Gregory Butte
7,705ft

La Verkin Creek

Langston Mountain
7,408ft

Kolob Peak
8,933ft

The Hardscrabble

UPPER KOLOB PLATEAU

Blue Springs Reservoir

Hop Valley

Burnt Mountain
7,682ft

To St. George and Las Vegas

Blackridge Wilderness Area

Hurricane Cliffs

Red Butte Wilderness Area

LOWER KOLOB PLATEAU

Firepit Knoll
7,265ft

Kolob Terrace

KOLOB TERRACE RD

Smith Mesa

Cave Valley

Lee Valley

North Guardian Angel
7,395ft

Keyhole Falls

I-15

La Verkin Creek

Hurricane Mesa

Left Fork

Tabernacle Dome
6,430ft

South Guardian Angel
7,140ft

Double Falls

Zion National Park

KOLOB TERRACE RD

Right Fork

North Creek

Cougar Mountain

Altar of Sacrifice
7,505ft

Rockville

The West Temple
7,810ft

Mount Kinesava
7,285ft

**SOUTH ENTRANCE**

Springdale

| HALF DAY | FULL DAY | AVOID THE CROWDS |
|---|---|---|
| **1** Zion Canyon Visitor Center | **1** Zion Canyon Visitor Center | **1** Kolob Canyons Visitor Center |
| **2** Court of the Patriarchs Viewpoint | **2** Zion Human History Museum | **2** Taylor Creek Trail |
| **3** Riverside Walk | **3** Riverside Walk | **3** Timber Creek Overlook Trail |
| **4** Lower Emerald Pool Trail | **4** The Narrows | **4** Kolob Canyons Viewpoint |
| **5** Zion Lodge | **5** Grotto Picnic Area | |
| | **6** Upper Emerald Pool Trail | |
| | **7** Zion Human History Museum | |
| | **8** Pa'rus Trail | |

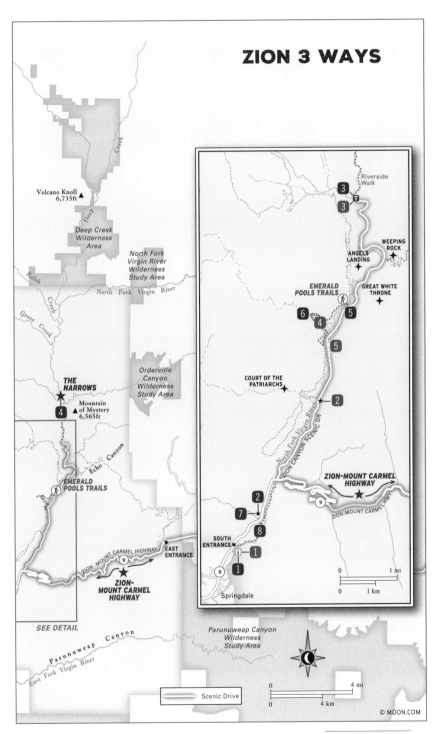

# ZION 3 WAYS

Volcano Knoll
6,735ft

Deep Creek
Wilderness
Area

North Fork
Virgin River
Wilderness
Study Area

North Fork Virgin River

Kolob Creek

Goose Creek

Orderville
Canyon
Wilderness
Study Area

**THE NARROWS**

Mountain
of Mystery
6,565ft

**4**

Echo Canyon

**EMERALD
POOLS TRAILS**

ZION-MOUNT CARMEL HIGHWAY   9

**ZION-
MOUNT CARMEL
HIGHWAY**

EAST
ENTRANCE

**SEE DETAIL**

Parunuweap Canyon

Parunuweap Canyon
Wilderness
Study Area

East Fork Virgin River

Scenic Drive

0                    4 mi
0                    4 km

---

Riverside
Walk

**3**

**3**  T

WEEPING
ROCK

ANGELS
LANDING

GREAT WHITE
THRONE

**EMERALD
POOLS TRAILS**

**6**   **4**   **5**

**5**

COURT OF THE
PATRIARCHS

**2**

North Fork Virgin River

ZION CANYON SCENIC DR

**ZION-MOUNT CARMEL
HIGHWAY**

9

ZION-MOUNT CARMEL HWY

**2**
**7**

**8**

SOUTH
ENTRANCE

**1**

**1**

9

Springdale

0                    1 mi
0                    1 km

© MOON.COM

# FULL DAY

An ideal full Zion day includes either trekking up Angels Landing (if you've secured a permit) or hiking part of the Narrows (itinerary below), which is the most constricted part of Zion Canyon. The latter involves hiking in the river, which, depending on the time of year, will be ankle- to waist-deep. Hiking poles or a sturdy stick and shoes with grippy soles go a long way. Note that the Narrows is off limits during high-water periods, usually in early spring.

**1** Start your day in Zion Canyon before sunrise, parking at the **Zion Canyon Visitor Center.**

**2** Walk the paved Pa'rus Trail to **Zion Human History Museum.** It won't be open yet, but its back patio is one of the park's best places to watch the sun's first rays strike the West Temple, the Towers of the Virgin, and the red-stained Altar of Sacrifice.

**3** Catch the shuttle from the museum or the visitor center (or plan ahead and rent an e-bike in Springdale). Exit at Temple of Sinawava and walk the 1-mile-long (1.6-km) **Riverside Walk** to the Narrows.

**4** At the start of **the Narrows,** wade into the river and walk upstream into a steep-walled canyon. Hike up for an hour or two, then retrace your steps (or swimming strokes).

**5** After your hike, take the shuttle to the **Grotto Picnic Area** for a shaded picnic lunch, or get off at Zion Lodge and pick something up at the Castle Dome Café.

**6** After lunch, cross the road and hike Kayenta Trail to its junction with the **Upper Emerald Pool Trail.** Climb to the pretty green pool and hike back down the way you came. If you have enough time, take the additional trails to Middle and Lower Emerald Pools.

**7** Return to **Zion Human History Museum** to watch the park movie and browse the collection.

**8** Wander along the **Pa'rus Trail** as the sun sets.

# AVOID THE CROWDS

Zion Canyon gets all the love—and most of the crowds. For a quieter experience, head to the **Kolob Canyons** section of the park. The scenery here is different from that of Zion Canyon, with a series of parallel "finger canyons" digging into steep rock walls.

From Zion Canyon's main entrance, it's about a 50-minute (39.7 mi/64 km) drive northwest to Kolob Canyons. Nearby **St. George** or **Cedar City** both make good base camps for Kolob Canyons, with plenty of lodging and restaurants. **Kolob Canyons Road** is the scenic 5-mile (8.1-km) stretch through this part of the park. Bring **lunch** or some snacks, since there's no food available.

**1** From I-15, take exit 40 and briefly stop at the **Kolob Canyons Visitor Center.** You can pay the park entrance fee and get info on trail conditions, then continue on Kolob Canyons Road.

**2** From the visitor center, drive 2 miles (3.2 km) east to the trailhead for **Taylor Creek Trail** (5 mi/8.1 km round-trip), which meanders along the creek past historic homesteader cabins and ends at an awesome cave-like alcove framed by two arches.

**3** Back at Taylor Creek Trailhead, drive to Kolob Canyons Viewpoint at the end of the 5-mile (8.1-km) scenic drive. The **Timber Creek Overlook Trail** here climbs a steep 0.5 mile (0.8 km) to an overlook with sight lines as far as Zion's Kolob Terrace and the Grand Canyon's North Rim.

**4** Although the only camping in this area is in the backcountry, it's worth hanging around until evening. Sunset makes the cliffs glow red, and the **Kolob Canyons Viewpoint** picnic area is a brilliant place to gaze up at the Milky Way.

## More Spots with Fewer Crowds

• Lava Point, off Kolob Terrace Road (page 53)

• Canyon Overlook Trail in eastern Zion (page 67)

# HIGHLIGHTS

## ZION CANYON

During the busiest times (7am-6:15pm Sat.-Sun. Feb.-early Mar., 7am-7:30pm daily mid-Mar.-mid-May, 6am-8:15pm daily mid-May-Sept., 7am-6:30pm daily Oct., 8am-5:45pm Christmas week, hours vary year to year; see www.nps.gov/zion for up-to-date information), the 6-mile (9.7-km) Zion Canyon Scenic Drive is closed to private cars, and you must travel on the **Zion Canyon Shuttle** (90 minutes round-trip, free, buses run every 7-10 minutes). The Zion Canyon Shuttle includes nine stops oriented around popular sights, attractions, and trails; you can get on and off the bus as often as you want. The road ends at **Temple of Sinawava,** where the **Riverside Walk Trail** begins. Note that you can travel up **Zion Canyon Scenic Drive** by bicycle, and shuttles are required to wait to pass until you pull over.

### Zion Nature Center

*2pm-6pm daily Memorial Day-Labor Day*

At the northern end of South Campground, the Zion Nature Center offers programs for kids, including Junior Ranger activities for ages 6-12. Although there's no shuttle stop for the Nature Center, it's an easy walk along the **Pa'rus Trail** from the Zion Canyon Visitor Center. Programs focus on natural history topics like insects and bats. Many Junior Ranger activities can be done on your own—pick up a booklet ($1) at the visitor center bookstore.

### Zion Human History Museum

*Shuttle stop: Zion Human History Museum; 9am-6pm daily mid-Apr.-late May, 9am-7pm daily late*

Zion Canyon

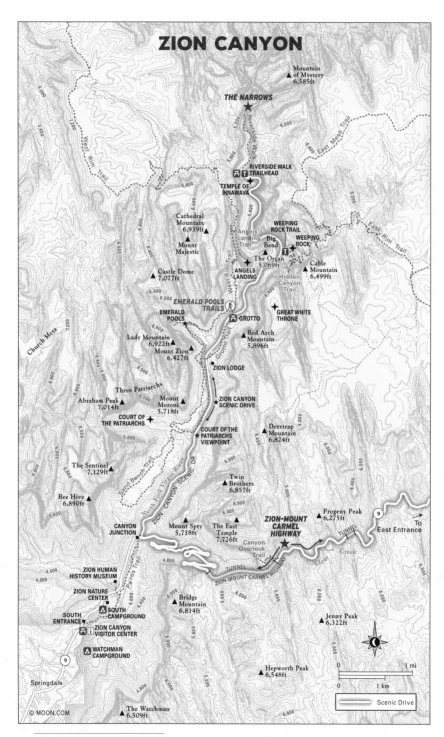

# ZION CANYON

Mountain of Mystery 6,585ft ▲

*THE NARROWS* ★

West Rim Trail

East Mesa Trail

Riverside Walk

🚻 🚹 RIVERSIDE WALK TRAILHEAD

TEMPLE OF SINAWAVA

Cathedral Mountain 6,939ft ▲

WEEPING ROCK TRAIL

Angels Landing Trail

Big Bend

WEEPING ROCK 🚹

Mount Majestic ▲

The Organ 5,069ft ▲

East Rim Trail

Castle Dome 7,077ft ▲

ANGELS LANDING

Cable Mountain 6,499ft ▲

Hidden Canyon Trail

West Rim Trail

*EMERALD POOLS TRAILS*

EMERALD POOLS ★

🚻 GROTTO

GREAT WHITE THRONE ▲

Lady Mountain 6,922ft ▲

Grotto Trail

Red Arch Mountain 5,896ft ▲

Mount Zion 6,427ft ▲

● ZION LODGE

Three Patriarchs

Abraham Peak 7,014ft ▲

Mount Moroni 5,718ft ▲

ZION CANYON SCENIC DRIVE

COURT OF THE PATRIARCHS ★

Deertrap Mountain 6,824ft ▲

COURT OF THE PATRIARCHS VIEWPOINT ★

Sand Bench Trail

The Sentinel 7,129ft ▲

Twin Brothers 6,857ft ▲

Bee Hive 6,890ft ▲

North Fork Virgin River

ZION CANYON SCENIC DR

*ZION-MOUNT CARMEL HIGHWAY*

Progeny Peak 6,275ft ▲

9

To East Entrance

CANYON JUNCTION

Mount Spry 5,718ft ▲

The East Temple 7,726ft ▲

Canyon Overlook Trail

★

TUNNEL

Creek

Pa'rus Trail

ZION HUMAN HISTORY MUSEUM ■

TUNNEL

ZION-MOUNT CARMEL HIGHWAY

ZION NATURE CENTER

SOUTH ENTRANCE 🔺 SOUTH CAMPGROUND

Bridge Mountain 6,814ft ▲

Jenny Peak 6,322ft ▲

🚻 ℹ ZION CANYON VISITOR CENTER

🔺 WATCHMAN CAMPGROUND

9

Springdale

Hepworth Peak 6,548ft ▲

N

0        1 mi

0        1 km

The Watchman 6,509ft ▲

© MOON.COM

━━━━━━ Scenic Drive

Since Zion Canyon is nestled between high rock walls, you won't actually see the sun set on the horizon. But the sandstone walls glowing red in the evening are just as enchanting as a good sunset. The **Pa'rus Trail** is a great place to stroll at twilight.

*May-early Sept., 9am-6pm daily early Sept.-early Oct., 10am-5pm Sat.-Sun. early Oct.-mid.-Apr.; entry included in park admission fee*
This museum explores the area's cultural history through an introductory film and historic exhibits about Indigenous people and Latter-day Saints. The museum is located at the first shuttle stop after the visitor center. It's a good place to visit when you're maxed out on hiking or if the weather forces you inside. From the museum's back patio, enjoy views of two tall peaks: **West Temple** and **Altar of Sacrifice,** so named because of the red iron streaks on its face. This patio is also a great spot to catch the sunrise.

## Court of the Patriarchs Viewpoint
*Shuttle stop: Court of the Patriarchs*
A very short trail from the shuttle stop leads to the view of the Patriarchs, a trio of peaks named, from left to right, Abraham, Isaac, and Jacob. Mount Moroni, the reddish peak on the far right, partially blocks the view of Jacob. Although the official viewpoint is a fine place to behold these peaks, you'll get an even better view if you cross the road and head about 0.5 mile (0.8 km) up **Sand Bench Trail.**

Court of the Patriarchs

### The Grotto
*Shuttle stop: The Grotto*
Positioned right along the riverbank with plenty of shade, the Grotto is a popular place for a picnic. From here, the **Grotto Trail** leads back to the lodge. Across the road, the **Kayenta Trail** links to the **Upper Emerald Pool Trail** and the **West Rim Trail,** which leads to **Angels Landing** and, eventually, to the **Kolob Terrace** section of the park.

### Weeping Rock
*Shuttle stop: Weeping Rock*
Several hikes start at Weeping Rock, including **Weeping Rock Trail,** which was closed 2019-2022 due to rockfall. The slab of Navajo sandstone that dropped 3,000 feet (914 m) from the side of Cable Mountain injured several visitors (all survived). A Utah Geological Survey report has found the area to be susceptible to large rockfall, and partial closures persist.

Weeping Rock is home to hanging gardens and many moisture-loving plants, including the striking Zion shooting star, which you can still peer at from behind the closure gate off the road. The rock "weeps" because this is a boundary between porous Navajo sandstone and denser Kayenta shale. Water trickles down through the sandstone, and when it can't penetrate the shale, it moves laterally to the face of the cliff. You can also see cables and rigging used by pioneers at this site in the early 1900s.

### Big Bend
*Shuttle stop: Big Bend*
Look up: This is where you're likely to see rock climbers on the towering walls or hikers on Angels Landing.

Zion Lodge (top); Big Bend (middle); waterfall at Weeping Rock (bottom)

## Temple of Sinawava

*Shuttle stop: Temple of Sinawava*

The last shuttle stop is at this sandstone amphitheater—named for a Paiute coyote spirit—that precedes the most drastic narrowing of Zion Canyon's 2,000-foot (610-m) walls. The paved wheelchair-accessible **Riverside Walk** (1 mi/1.6 km one-way) hugs the eastern side of the Virgin River up the canyon alongside hanging gardens and birds nesting in holes in the cliffs. This path terminates at **the Narrows,** where you have to wade (and sometimes swim, depending on water levels) the Virgin River to continue. Don't continue without proper footwear and gear.

## KOLOB TERRACE

The Kolob Terrace section of the park is a high plateau roughly parallel to and west of Zion Canyon. From the town of Virgin (15 mi/24 km west of the south entrance station on Hwy. 9), steep Kolob Terrace Road—paved, though unsuitable for trailers—runs north up a narrow stretch of land with drop-offs on either side before widening onto a high plateau. The **Hurricane Cliffs** rise from the west, while the back of Zion Canyon's walls lies to the east. The road passes in and out of the park, terminating at **Kolob Reservoir,** a popular boating and fishing destination outside the park. Snow usually blocks driving through the Kolob Terrace section in winter.

Temple of Sinawava

## Lava Point

The panorama from Lava Point (elev. 7,890 ft/2,405 m) takes in Cedar Breaks's hoodoos to the north, the Pink Cliffs to the northeast, Zion Canyon Narrows to the east, and Arizona's Mount Trumbull to the south. Sitting atop a lava flow, Lava Point is a good place to cool off—temperatures are about 20 degrees Fahrenheit (11 degrees C) cooler than in Zion Canyon—and filled with aspens, ponderosa pines, Gambel oaks, and white firs. A small primitive campground near the point offers free sites during the warmer months. From Virgin, take Kolob Terrace Road about 21 miles (34 km) north to Lava Point turnoff; the viewpoint is 1.8 miles (2.9 km) farther on a well-marked, unpaved spur road. Vehicles longer than 19 feet (5.8 m) are prohibited on Lava Point road. The trip from Virgin to Lava Point takes about an hour.

Lava Point

# SCENIC DRIVES

## ZION CANYON SCENIC DRIVE

**DRIVING DISTANCE:** 7.9 miles (12.7 km) one-way
**DRIVING TIME:** 30 minutes one-way
**START:** Zion Canyon Visitor Center
**END:** Temple of Sinawava

Zion Canyon Scenic Drive winds through the canyon floor along the North Fork of the Virgin River, past some of the most spectacular scenery in the park, including **the Patriarchs, Weeping Rock,** and the **Temple of Sinawava.** Also visible from several points along Zion Canyon Drive is the **Great White Throne.** Topping out at 6,744 feet (2,056 m), this bulky chunk of Navajo sandstone has become emblematic of the park. Ride the shuttle in the evening to watch the rock change color in the light of the setting sun.

A **shuttle bus** ferries visitors along this route spring-fall, when it is for the most part closed to private cars. Hiking trails branch off to sweeping viewpoints and narrow side canyons. Water-loving adventurers can continue past the pavement's end and hike up the Virgin River through **the Narrows** of upper Zion Canyon.

## ★ ZION-MOUNT CARMEL HIGHWAY

**DRIVING DISTANCE:** 24.5 miles (39 km) one-way
**DRIVING TIME:** 2 hours one-way
**START:** Zion Canyon Visitor Center
**END:** Mount Carmel Junction

The east section of the park is a land of sandstone slickrock, hoodoos, and narrow canyons. You can get a good eyeful of the dramatic scenery along Zion-Mount Carmel Highway (Hwy. 9) between Zion Canyon Visitor Center and the east entrance station. Highlights on the plateau include the Canyon Overlook Trail, which begins just east of the long tunnel, and the bizarre Checkerboard Mesa, near the east entrance station.

- **Mile 0:** Zion Canyon Visitor Center
- **Mile 1.6:** Canyon Junction; 1.6 miles (2.5 km) from the visitor center. Highway 9 turns east here

---

Great White Throne (left); Zion-Mount Carmel Tunnel (right)

# NAVAJO SANDSTONE

Zion Canyon's 1,600-2,200-foot (488-671-m) cliffs of Navajo sandstone were formed from immense sand dunes deposited during a hot dry period about 200 million years ago. Shifting winds blew the sand in one direction, then another—the resulting diagonal lines are called **cross-bedding.**

When these dunes were forming, the landmass beneath was positioned about 15 degrees north of the equator, approximately where Honduras is located today, according to University of Nebraska-Lincoln researchers. The shift patterns in the sandstone—the slanting striations noticeable in the cliff faces—were caused in part by intense monsoon rains, which compacted and moved the dunes.

Navajo sandstone

Eventually, a shallow sea washed over the dunes. Lapping waves left shells behind, and as the shells dissolved, their lime seeped down into the sand and cemented it into sandstone. After the Colorado Plateau lifted, rivers cut deeply through the sandstone layer. The formation's lower layers are stained red from iron oxides.

The east side of Zion, especially Checkerboard Mesa, is a great place to view the warps and striations in the sandstone. But with the right light and a pair of binoculars, you can see cross-bedding on Zion Canyon's big walls too. The mostly white Navajo sandstone Great White Throne is a good feature on which to observe this.

and begins to climb from the floor of Zion Canyon through a series of six switchbacks to a high plateau. Pullouts provide views of the canyon below.

- **Mile 3.3:** Stop at an overlook pullout on the left side of the road to catch views of the Great Arch of Zion.

- **Mile 5:** Zion-Mount Carmel Tunnel. This narrow 1.1-mile (1.8-km) tunnel, completed in 1930,

offers glimpses of park scenery through several windows cut into the tunnel wall. Any vehicle more than 7 feet, 10 inches (2.4 m) wide, 11 feet, 4 inches (3.5 m) high, or 40 feet (12.1 m) long (50 ft/15.2 m with a trailer) must be escorted through in one-way traffic; a $15 fee charged on-site gets you two passages. Park staff will stop oncoming traffic, allowing you enough time to drive down the middle of the tunnel, but you don't actually follow an escort vehicle. Hours for large vehicles are limited (8am-8pm daily Apr.-Sept., 8am-4:30pm daily Nov.-Mar., hours may vary year to year, more information at 435/772-3256, www.nps.gov/zion). A much shorter (530-ft/162-m) tunnel to the east is easy to navigate and requires no special considerations.

- **Mile 6.1:** Canyon Overlook Trail. Just past the eastern end of the tunnel, this 1-mile (1.6-km) round-trip trail leads to a viewpoint overlooking Zion Canyon.

- **Mile 10.9:** Checkerboard Mesa. This striking feature is visible from the road, but pull off to admire its distinctive pattern, caused by a combination of vertical fractures and horizontal bedding planes, both accentuated by weathering.

- **Mile 11:** East entrance. A pay station with no services.

- **Mile 24.5:** Mount Carmel Junction. From here, U.S. 89 heads north to Bryce Canyon National Park or south to Kanab.

## KOLOB CANYONS ROAD

**DRIVING DISTANCE:** 5 miles (8.1 km) one-way
**DRIVING TIME:** 20-30 minutes one-way
**START:** Kolob Canyons Visitor Center
**END:** Kolob Canyons Viewpoint

This paved 5-mile (8.1-km) scenic drive begins at the **Kolob Canyons Visitor Center** (3752 E. Kolob Canyons Rd., New Harmony; 435/772-3256; 8am-5pm daily mid-Mar.-mid-Oct., 8am-4:30pm

Checkerboard Mesa (top); the Zion-Mount Carmel Highway descends into the park (middle); Kolob Canyons (bottom)

daily mid-Oct.-mid-Mar.) just off I-15. It winds past the Kolob's dramatic Finger Canyons to the Timber Creek Overlook Trail. The first part of the drive follows the 200-mile-long (320-km) Hurricane Fault, which forms the west edge of the Markagunt Plateau. Look for the tilted rock layers deformed by friction as the plateau rose nearly 1 mile (1.6 km). The **Taylor Creek Trail,** which begins 2 miles (3.2 km) past the visitor center, provides a close look at the canyons. At the Lee Pass trailhead, 4 miles (6.4 km) beyond the visitor center, **La Verkin Creek Trail** takes you to **Kolob Arch** and beyond. Signs at the end of the road identify the buttes, mesas, and mountains.

Lee Pass is named for John D. Lee, who was the only person ever convicted in the Mountain Meadows Massacre. Lee is said to have lived nearby for a spell after the 1857 incident, in which an alliance of Latter-day Saints and Native Americans attacked a California-bound wagon train, killing about 120 people. Only children too young to tell the story were spared. The Latter-day Saint community tried to cover up the incident and hindered federal attempts to apprehend the killers. Only Lee, who oversaw Native American affairs in southern Utah at the time, was ever brought to justice; he was later executed.

# BEST HIKES

## ZION CANYON
### Pa'rus Trail
**DISTANCE:** 3.5 miles (5.6 km) round-trip
**DURATION:** 2 hours round-trip
**ELEVATION GAIN:** 50 feet (15 m)
**EFFORT:** Easy
**TRAILHEADS:** South Campground and Canyon Junction
**SHUTTLE STOPS:** Zion Canyon Visitor Center and Canyon Junction

This paved, wheelchair-accessible trail runs from **South Campground** near the visitor center to the **Canyon Junction** shuttle stop. Meandering around the Virgin River, it makes for a nice early-morning or evening stroll or bike ride. Listen for the trilling song of the canyon wren (easy to hear), then try to spot the small bird in the bushes (not so easy). The mostly flat Pa'rus Trail is the only trail in the park open to bicycles and pets.

## West Rim Trail to Angels Landing
**DISTANCE:** 5.4 miles (8.7 km) round-trip
**DURATION:** 4 hours round-trip
**ELEVATION GAIN:** 1,488 feet (454 m)
**EFFORT:** Strenuous
**TRAILHEAD:** Across the road from Grotto Picnic Area
**SHUTTLE STOP:** The Grotto
**PERMIT REQUIRED**

This strenuous trail leads to some of the best views of Zion Canyon. From **the Grotto** (elev. 4,300 ft/1,311 m), cross the footbridge, then turn right along the river. The trail, which was blasted out of the cliff side by the Civilian Conservation Corps in the 1930s, climbs up into the shady depths of the aptly named **Refrigerator Canyon. Walter's Wiggles,** 21 closely spaced switchbacks, wind up to a trail junction and **Scout Lookout,** with excellent canyon views. If you turn around here, your hike will be 4 miles (6.4 km) round-trip and gain 1,050 feet (320 m) in elevation. If you continue, it's a daunting 0.5 mile (0.8 km) to the summit of Angels Landing.

**Angels Landing** itself is a sheer-walled monolith 1,500 feet (457 m) above the North Fork of the Virgin River. Although the trail to the **summit** is rough and very narrow, chains provide security on the sections with high exposure. Hike this final approach to Angels Landing carefully and only in good weather; don't go if the trail is covered with snow or ice or if thunderstorms threaten. Children must be closely supervised, and anyone afraid of heights should skip this trail. Once on top, the panorama makes the effort worthwhile. Not surprisingly, it's best to do this steep hike during the cooler morning hours. Start extra-early to avoid the crowds, which can make the final stretch all the more frightening.

Note that the park is piloting a **permit** program (my best guess is that this will become permanent), so anyone who wishes to hike any part of the trail must obtain a permit. There's a seasonal lottery system ($3 pp, apply 1-3 months in advance, specific seasonal lottery windows listed at www.nps.gov/zion). You can also try your luck at getting a next-day permit ($6 pp); apply by 3pm the day before you want the permit. Both permit types are available at www.recreation.gov.

## Weeping Rock Trail
**DISTANCE:** 0.5 mile (0.8 km) round-trip
**DURATION:** 30 minutes round-trip
**ELEVATION GAIN:** 100 feet (30 m)
**EFFORT:** Easy
**TRAILHEAD:** Weeping Rock parking area
**SHUTTLE STOP:** Weeping Rock

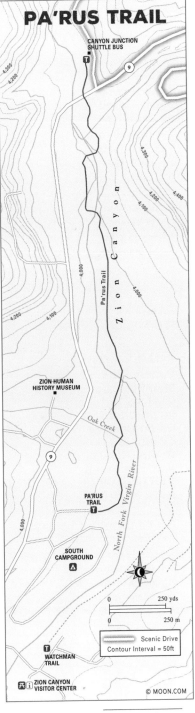

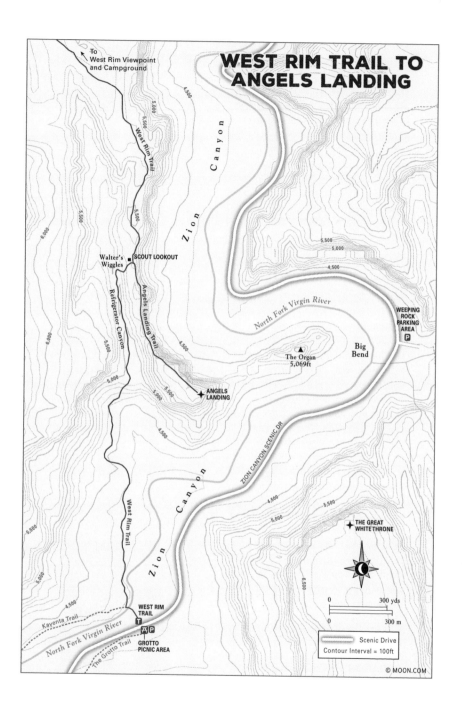

# WEST RIM TRAIL TO ANGELS LANDING

To West Rim Viewpoint and Campground

West Rim Trail

Zion Canyon

Walter's Wiggles
SCOUT LOOKOUT

Refrigerator Canyon

Angels Landing Trail

North Fork Virgin River

WEEPING ROCK PARKING AREA

The Organ 5,069ft

Big Bend

ANGELS LANDING

ZION CANYON SCENIC DR

Zion Canyon

West Rim Trail

THE GREAT WHITE THRONE

Kayenta Trail

WEST RIM TRAIL

North Fork Virgin River

The Grotto Trail

GROTTO PICNIC AREA

5,000 / 5,500 / 6,000 / 4,500 / 6,500

| 0 | 300 yds |
| 0 | 300 m |

Scenic Drive
Contour Interval = 100ft

© MOON.COM

This easy trail winds past lush vegetation and wildflowers to a series of cliff-side springs above an overhang. The springs emerge where water seeping through more than 2,000 feet (610 m) of Navajo sandstone meets a layer of impervious shale.

**Note:** This was the site of a major rockfall in 2019 that forced the long-term closure of the trail. Check its status before planning to hike here.

## Hidden Canyon Trail

**DISTANCE:** 3 miles (4.8 km) round-trip
**DURATION:** 2.5-3 hours round-trip
**ELEVATION GAIN:** 850 feet (259 m)
**EFFORT:** Strenuous
**TRAILHEAD:** Weeping Rock parking area
**SHUTTLE STOP:** Weeping Rock

See if you can spot the entrance to Hidden Canyon from below. Inside the narrow canyon are small sandstone caves, a little natural arch, and diverse plantlife. The high walls, rarely more than 65 feet (20 m) apart, block sunlight except for a short time at midday. From the trailhead at the Weeping Rock parking area, follow the East Rim Trail 0.8 mile (1.3 km) up the cliff face, then turn right and go 0.7 mile (1.1 km) on the Hidden Canyon Trail to the canyon entrance. Footing can be a bit difficult in places, but chains provide handholds on the exposed sections. Steps chopped into the rock just inside Hidden Canyon help bypass some deep pools. After heavy rains and spring runoff, the creek forms a small waterfall at the canyon entrance. The canyon itself is about 1 mile (1.6 km) long and mostly easy walking, although the trail fades away. Look for the arch on the right about 0.5 mile (0.8 km) up the canyon.

**Note:** The Weeping Rock trailhead was the site of a major rockfall in 2019 that forced the long-term closure of this trail. Check its status before planning to hike here.

Pa'rus Trail

# TOP HIKE
# EMERALD POOLS TRAILS

**DISTANCE:** 4 miles (6.4 km) round-trip
**DURATION:** 2 hours round-trip
**ELEVATION GAIN:** 350 feet (107 m)
**EFFORT:** Moderate
**TRAILHEAD:** Across the footbridge from the Grotto
**SHUTTLE STOP:** The Grotto

Pools, small waterfalls, and views of Zion Canyon make this hike a favorite. The trail begins at the **Grotto,** crosses a footbridge, and turns left onto **Kay-**

EMERALD POOLS TRAILS

5,600
5,600
5,800
5,200
4,800
EMERALD POOLS TRAILS
THE GROTTO PICNIC AREA
Upper Emerald Pool Trail
Middle Emerald Pool
Upper Emerald Pool
Lower Emerald Pool
Kayenta Trail
North Fork Virgin River
ZION CANYON SCENIC DRIVE
Lower Emerald Pool Trail
Middle Emerald Pool Trail
4,400
6,800
4,800
5,200
5,600
Lady Mountain ▲ 6,922ft
ZION CANYON SCENIC DR.
Grotto Trail
4,400
6,800
▲ Mount Zion 6,427ft
4,800
5,200
5,600
ZION LODGE
6,400
6,000
5,600
5,200
Sand Bench Trail

0        300 yds
0        300 m

Scenic Drive
Contour Interval = 80ft

© MOON.COM

**enta Trail,** which you'll climb for 1 mile (1.6 km), gaining views of Zion Canyon below. At the end of Kayenta Trail is the **Middle Emerald Pool,** where you can access well-marked short trails to the Upper Pool (0.5 mi/0.8 km) and the Lower Pool (0.6 mi/1 km). Visit them in any order. The 4-mile (6.4-km) round-trip distance for this hike includes hiking to all three pools via Kayenta Trail.

**Upper Emerald Pool** resembles a mini beach scene, with folks wading in the shallow water and picnicking in the sand. **Lower Emerald Pool** offers the most visually unique experience—a trail passes under an overhanging rock with water dripping or spraying down it, depending on how wet the year has been. Below, you'll be able to spot the pool. True to their name, all three pools have a greenish tint, some more than others, thanks to the algae inhabiting them.

Although the Emerald Pool trails are relatively easy, there are steep rocky steps, and parts of the trail can get icy and slippery any time of year. Several people have died in falls on the Emerald Pool trails, so hike with caution.

## Riverside Walk
**DISTANCE:** 2.2 miles (3.5 km) round-trip
**DURATION:** 1-2 hours round-trip
**ELEVATION GAIN:** 57 feet (17 m)
**EFFORT:** Easy
**TRAILHEAD:** Temple of Sinawava parking area
**SHUTTLE STOP:** Temple of Sinawava

One of the most popular and easiest hikes in the park, this nearly level paved trail begins at the end of Zion Canyon Scenic Drive and heads upstream along the Virgin River to the Narrows. While you can complete the walk quickly, allow a little more time to take in the hanging gardens, explore the riverbank in accessible spots, and cool off in the shallow water. Countless springs and seeps on the canyon walls support plants and swamps, attracting wildlife like squirrels and deer. Most springs occur at the boundary between the porous Navajo sandstone and the less permeable Kayenta Formation below. At trail's end, the canyon is wide enough only for the river. To continue, you must wade with waterproof high-traction footwear—and sometimes even swim. Riverside Walk is wheelchair accessible, though there can be a few spots with slick, uneven terrain.

## ★ The Narrows
**DISTANCE:** 9.4 miles (15.1 km) round-trip
**DURATION:** 8 hours round-trip
**ELEVATION GAIN:** 200 feet (61 m)
**EFFORT:** Strenuous
**TRAILHEAD:** End of Riverside Walk
**SHUTTLE STOP:** Temple of Sinawava

Upper Zion Canyon is the most famous backcountry area in the park, and among the most strenuous. There's no trail, and significant wading or swimming is required,

a hiker on Angels Landing (top); Weeping Rock waterfall (middle); columbine in The Narrows (bottom)

Riverside Walk

sometimes knee- to chest-deep. At the canyon's narrowest, the high fluted walls are only 20 feet (6 m) apart, and little sunlight penetrates the depths. Mysterious side canyons beckon. The haunting lighting, the sense of adventure required to navigate the canyon, and otherworldly hanging gardens make this hike worth the hype.

To hike the Narrows bottom up, hikers should be well outfitted and in good shape—river hiking is more tiring than land hiking. Hazards include flash floods and hypothermia; even in summer, expect water temperatures of about 68°F (20°C) and around 38°F (3°C) in winter. Finding the best time to go can be tricky. In spring, runoff is usually too high. Summer thunderstorms bring toxic cyanobacteria blooms (which means keeping water away from your face, or avoiding contact altogether if toxicity is too high) and flash-flood risks that can temporarily close the hike altogether. In winter,

the water is too cold, unless you're in a dry suit. Early summer (mid-June–mid-July) and early autumn (mid-Sept.–mid-Oct.) are the best windows.

What exactly does "bottom up" mean? Hiking the Narrows this way means navigating it south to north, starting from the main Zion Canyon. The benefits of doing so are easy access, no permit required, few technical challenges, and a length that can be knocked out in a day. The downside is that most people hike the Narrows this way, so you'll deal with more crowds, especially toward the beginning. Hiking the Narrows from the top down is a two-day adventure requiring an overnight permit. Top-down access is via a remote road, and you may need to book a guide if you lack the navigation skills to confidently execute this adventure independently.

Don't be tempted to wear river sandals or sneakers up the Narrows; it's easy to twist an ankle on

The Narrows

the slippery rocks. You can use hiking boots you don't mind drenching, but the ideal solution is available from **Zion Adventures** (36 Lion Blvd., Springdale; 435/772-1001; www.zionadventures.com) and other Springdale outfitters. They rent specialized river-hiking boots, along with neoprene socks, hiking poles, and, in cool weather, dry pants and dry suits. Boots, socks, and sticks rent for $29; with a dry suit, the package costs $59. They also offer guidance on hiking the Narrows and lead tours of the section below Orderville Canyon ($279-309 pp, varies by season). **Zion Outfitter** (7 Zion Park Blvd., Springdale; 435/772-5090; www.zionoutfitter.com), located just outside the park entrance, and **Zion Guru** (795 Zion Park Blvd., Springdale; 435/632-0432; www.zionguru.com) provide similar services at comparable prices.

Before your hike, check conditions and the forecast with rangers at the Zion Canyon Visitor Center—they can also provide pointers and a handout with useful information. No permit is needed if you're not going farther than Big Springs.

For a half-day trip, follow the Narrows 1.5 miles (2.4 km, about 2 hours) upstream from the end of the **Riverside Walk** to **Orderville Canyon,** then back the same way. Orderville Canyon makes a good destination itself since it attracts less hoopla than Zion Canyon, isn't very difficult to canyoneer, and is arguably just as beautiful. This canyon can be accessed via a side road off Kolob Terrace Road. A permit is required to explore this area beyond the first 0.25 mile (0.4 km). In the main canyon of the Narrows, day hikers without permits must turn around at

**Big Springs,** about 2.5 miles (4 km) past Orderville.

# EAST OF ZION CANYON
## Canyon Overlook Trail
**DISTANCE:** 1 mile (1.6 km) round-trip
**DURATION:** 1 hour round-trip
**ELEVATION GAIN:** 163 feet (50 m)
**EFFORT:** Easy
**TRAILHEAD:** Parking area just east of the long (westernmost) tunnel on the Zion-Mount Carmel Highway

This fun hike starts on the road east of Zion Canyon and features great views without the stiff climbs found on many Zion trails. The trail winds along the ledges of **Pine Creek Canyon,** which opens into a valley. Panoramas at trail's end take in lower Zion Canyon in the distance, including the 580-foot-high (177-m) **Great Arch of Zion**—termed a "blind arch" because it's open only on one side. On a busy day, finding parking in the lot can be more challenging than the hike itself.

Canyon Overlook Trail

Timber Creek Overlook Trail (left); Double Arch Alcove at the end of Taylor Creek Trail (right)

## KOLOB CANYONS
### Taylor Creek Trail
**DISTANCE:** 5 miles (8.1 km) round-trip
**DURATION:** 4 hours round-trip
**ELEVATION GAIN:** 450 feet (137 m)
**EFFORT:** Easy-moderate
**TRAILHEAD:** 2 miles (3.2 km) east of Kolob Canyons Visitor Center, left side of the road

This excellent day hike from Kolob Canyons Road heads upstream along the **Middle Fork of Taylor Creek**. **Double Arch Alcove** is 2.7 miles (4.3 km) from the trailhead; you could continue on, but 350 yards (320 m) past the arch, a giant rockfall that occurred in 1990 blocks the way. Along the way, you'll enjoy easy creek crossings, decent shade, smatterings of wildflowers, and two historic cabins. From this trail, you can also explore the **North Fork of Taylor Creek.**

### Timber Creek Overlook Trail
**DISTANCE:** 1 mile (1.6 km) round-trip
**DURATION:** 30 minutes round-trip
**ELEVATION GAIN:** 100 feet (30 m)
**EFFORT:** Easy-moderate
**TRAILHEAD:** At the end of Kolob Canyons Road, 5 miles (8.1 km) from the visitor center

This short but relatively steep, rocky jaunt from the parking lot at the road's end leads to **Timber Creek Overlook,** where you'll find the best panoramic views of Kolob Canyons. On a clear day, the North Rim of the Grand Canyon is even visible from the overlook.

# BACKPACKING

A few longer trails in Zion make great overnight trips. From the Kolob Terrace Road's Lee Pass trailhead, the **La Verkin Creek Trail to Kolob Arch** is about 6.5 miles (10.5 km), with several backcountry campsites along the way. For a longer backpacking trip, the popular 16.2-mile (26-km) **West Rim Trail** starts from Lava Point on Kolob Terrace Road and descends to West Rim trailhead, across from the Grotto in Zion Canyon. West Rim

## ROCK CLIMBING IN ZION

rock climbing in Zion

In spring and fall, rock climbers come to scale Zion's high Navajo sandstone cliffs, which are popular among big-wall alpinists. Especially after rainfall, the sandstone is fragile, prone to crumbling and flaking. This is not a beginner-friendly climbing area—experience with crack climbing on lead using trad (traditional) protection is a must.

To catch a glimpse of Zion's climbers, look up at the crags around **Big Bend** in Zion Canyon.

can also be backpacked as a shuttle if you can arrange a ride back to the starting trailhead.

### PERMITS

When planning a trip, check the park's website to learn about trails, find backcountry campsites, and reserve a permit (see www.zionpermits.nps.gov; $5 reservation fee, $15-25 permit depending on group size). The day before your trip, convert your reservation into a permit online by emailing zion_park_information@nps.gov.

# BIKING

One of the fringe benefits of the Zion Canyon shuttle bus is the great bicycling that has resulted from the lack of car traffic. It used to be a little harrowing to bike along the narrow traffic-choked **Zion Canyon Scenic Drive,** but now it's a joy. When the shuttle buses get crowded (and they do), biking is a great way to explore the canyon.

On the stretch of road where cars are permitted—between the Zion Canyon Visitor Center and Canyon Junction (where the Zion-Mount

## ZION NATIONAL PARK FOOD OPTIONS

| NAME | LOCATION | TYPE |
|------|----------|------|
| **Red Rock Grill** | Zion Lodge | sit-down restaurant |
| **Castle Dome Café** | Zion Lodge | snack bar |

Carmel Highway meets Zion Canyon Scenic Drive)—the 2-mile (3.2-km) paved **Pa'rus Trail** is open to cyclists as well as pedestrians and makes for easy stress-free pedaling. Bicycles are allowed on the park road, but they must pull over to allow shuttle buses to pass.

If you decide you've had enough cycling, every shuttle bus has a rack that can hold two bicycles. Bike parking is plentiful at the visitor center, Zion Lodge, and most trailheads.

Outside the Zion Canyon area, **Kolob Terrace Road** is a good place to stretch your legs; it's 22 miles (35 km) to Kolob Reservoir.

There's no place to mountain bike off-road within the park.

## RENTALS

Three-speed cruiser bikes are available in Springdale at **Zion Outfitter** (7 Zion Park Blvd.; 435/772-5090; http://zionoutfitter.com; 7am-9pm daily). **Zion Adventures** (36 Lion Blvd., Springdale; 435/772-1001; www.zionadventures.com; 8am-8pm daily Mar.-Oct., 8am-7pm daily Nov., 9am-7pm daily Dec.-Feb.) rents road bikes ($35 per day) and e-bikes ($60 per day), both of which are good for park roads. **Zion Cycles** (868 Zion Park Blvd., Springdale; 435/772-0400; www.zioncycles.com; 9am-6pm daily), tucked behind Zion Pizza Noodle, has similar rentals.

bikers pedaling Zion Canyon Scenic Drive (left); La Verkin Creek Trail (right)

| FOOD | PRICE | HOURS |
|------|-------|-------|
| Southwestern | moderate | 7am-11am, 11:30am-8pm daily |
| fast food | budget | 7:30am-4pm daily spring-fall |

# HORSEBACK RIDING

Trail rides on horses and mules leave from the **corral near Zion Lodge** (435/679-8665; www.canyonrides.com; Mar.-Oct.) and head down the Virgin River. A one-hour trip ($50) goes to the Court of the Patriarchs, and a half-day ride ($100) follows the Sand Bench Trail. Riders must be at least age 7 for the short ride and age 10 for the half-day ride, and riders can weigh no more than 220 pounds.

# FOOD AND LODGING

Within the park, Zion Lodge is the only place to get food or a room for the night. Look to Springdale or closer to the east entrance of the park for more options.

## ZION LODGE

*Shuttle stop: Zion Lodge; 435/772-7700 or 888/297-2757; www.zionlodge.com*

Rustic Zion Lodge is in the heart of Zion Canyon, 3 miles (4.8 km) up Zion Canyon Scenic Drive. Open year-round, Zion Lodge provides the only accommodations and food options within the park. Reservations can be made up to 13 months in advance, and spring-fall it's typically booked out many months in advance. There are four accessible rooms (two with grab bars, two with roll-in showers) and a wheelchair is available for loan. Motel rooms and cabins (gas fireplaces, no TVs)

near the main lodge are a little less expensive.

Dine inside the lodge at the **Red Rock Grill** (435/772-7760; dinner reservations required; 7am-8pm daily; dinner entrées $13-21), featuring a Southwestern and Native

Zion Lodge

# ZION NATIONAL PARK CAMPGROUNDS

| NAME | LOCATION | SEASON | SITES AND AMENITIES |
|---|---|---|---|
| Watchman Campground | Zion Canyon | year-round | 197 sites, 65 with electrical hookups ($30) |
| South Campground | Zion Canyon | Mar.-Oct. | 128 sites |
| Lava Point Campground | Kolob Terrace Road | May-Sept. | 6 sites |

American-influenced menu for breakfast (6:30am-11:30am), lunch (11:30am-5pm), and dinner (5pm-9pm) daily. There's also snack bar called the **Castle Dome Café** (breakfast and lunch daily spring-fall) with fast food and a patio beer garden cart.

The lodge also has evening programs, a gift shop, Wi-Fi in the lobby (not high-speed), and accessible public restrooms.

## BEST PICNIC SPOTS
### The Grotto
*Shuttle stop: The Grotto*
This shady picnic area is Zion's best, with fire grates, lots of picnic tables, water, and restrooms. From here, the 0.5-mile (0.8-km) Grotto Trail goes to Zion Lodge (where you can grab some food from the snack bar). The Grotto itself is just a pleasant clearing, but two of the park's most popular trails (leading to Upper Emerald Pool and Angels Landing) start just across the road. Near this trailhead, you can also perch along the shores of the Virgin River for a snack.

### Riverside Walk
*Shuttle stop: Temple of Sinawava*
Although it's not a formal picnic area, benches along the path offer an opportunity to watch birds nesting or feeding in the sandstone cliff. There's also wildlife-viewing (mostly deer) in the Virgin River. At the shuttle stop, there's also a restroom and potable water for refilling your hydration pack or bottles.

### Visitor Center Parking Area
*Shuttle stop: Zion Canyon Visitor Center*
Not the most pleasant picnic spot, but what it lacks in tranquility, it makes up for in convenience. If you need to pick up a lunch, take the short walk into Springdale and you'll find a good café almost immediately.

### ★ Kolob Canyons Viewpoint
The views from this small, fairly primitive, and quieter picnic area stretch to the North Rim of the Grand Canyon. Hike the 1-mile (1.6-km) round-trip Timber Creek Overlook Trail for even more views. Be sure to fill your water bottle at the Kolob

| RV LIMIT | PRICE | RESERVATIONS |
|---|---|---|
| 61 (no generators permitted) | $20 | yes |
| 120 permit RVs, no hookups | $20 | yes |
| vehicles longer than 19 feet (5.7 m) prohibited | $20 | no |

Canyons Visitor Center (and don't expect flush toilets at the viewpoint).

This viewpoint in the Kolob Canyons section of the park is not served by the shuttle. From the Kolob Canyons Visitor Center, drive 5 miles (8.1 km) to the end of the Kolob Canyons Road.

# CAMPING

----------------------------------------

Campgrounds in the park often fill up during Easter and other major holidays. During summer they're often full by early afternoon, so it's best to arrive early in the day. The South and Watchman Campgrounds, both just inside the south entrance, have sites with water but no showers.

Up Kolob Terrace Road are six first-come, first-served sites at Lava Point Campground.

Watchman Campground

# INFORMATION AND SERVICES

## Entrance Stations

*$35 per vehicle, $30 motorcyclists, $20 pedestrians or bicyclists, admission good for 7 days and unlimited shuttle use*

### East Entrance Station

*Zion-Mount Carmel Highway (Hwy. 9)*
From the east, you enter the park via Zion-Mount Carmel Highway (Hwy. 9) and pass through a long tunnel before popping into Zion Canyon a couple of miles north of the visitor center.

### South Entrance Station

*Hwy. 9, Springdale*
From Springdale, you enter the south end of Zion Canyon, near the visitor center and the Zion Canyon shuttle buses.

### Kolob Terrace Road Entrance

*Kolob Terrace Road*
From the tiny town of Virgin and Highway 9, head north on Kolob Terrace Road to explore this less traveled part of the park, with access to backcountry trails.

## Visitor Centers

### Zion Canyon Visitor Center

*435/772-3256; 8am-6pm daily mid-Apr.-late May and Sept.-mid-Oct., 8am-7pm daily late May-Aug., 8am-5pm daily mid-Oct.-early-Apr.*
The park's sprawling Zion Canyon Visitor Center is a hub of activity. The plaza outside the building features good interpretive plaques with enough info to get you going on a hike. Inside, a large area is devoted to backcountry information, and rangers can answer questions about trails, give weather forecast updates, and help arrange shuttles to remote trailheads. The wilderness desk (435/772-0170) opens at 7am daily late April-late November, an hour earlier than the rest of the visitor centers. A Backcountry Shuttle Board allows hikers to coordinate transportation between trailheads.

The busiest part of the visitor center is the bookstore, stocked with an excellent selection of books covering natural history, human history, and regional travel. Topographic and geologic maps, posters, and postcards are also sold here.

### Kolob Canyons Visitor Center

*I-15; 435/772-3256; 8am-5pm daily mid-Mar.-early Oct., 8am-4:30pm daily mid-Oct.-mid-Mar.*
Just off I-15 exit 90, the Kolob Canyons Visitor Center serves as the entrance station to this section of the park. Although it's small and has just a handful of exhibits, the Kolob Canyons Visitor Center is a good place to get information on exploring the Kolob area. Hikers can learn about current trail conditions and obtain permits required for overnight trips and Zion Narrows day trips.

# TRANSPORTATION

## Getting There

### Car

Zion National Park is 86 miles (138 km) southwest of Bryce Canyon National Park. From Bryce, take Highway 12 west for 13.5 miles (21.7 km) to its junction with U.S. 89. Turn south on U.S. 89 and follow it 43 miles (69 km) to Mount Carmel Junction and Highway 9. Turn right (west) here and travel 13 miles (21.7 km) to the east entrance of Zion. Expect this drive to take 1.5-2 hours.

Once in the park, the Zion-Mount Carmel Highway (Hwy. 9) goes across a high plateau, through two tunnels (one is 1 mi/1.6 km long), and down a series of switchbacks to Zion Canyon.

## Parking

The visitor center parking lot fills up early and stays full all day. If you get to the lot before 8am-9am or after 5pm-6pm, there may be parking spaces available. Campers and lodge guests can drive to their overnight spots and park there. Midday visitors staying in Springdale should stay parked at their lodging and catch the Zion-Springdale shuttle to the edge of the park (or walk or bike into the park). Springdale also has parking lots and some on-street parking (fees charged everywhere).

### Zion-Springdale Shuttle

*mid-Mar.-Nov., runs every 10-15 minutes, starting at 7am during peak season; seasonal hours vary year-to-year; no pets allowed; free*

During the high season, one line of the Zion Canyon shuttle bus travels between Springdale and the park entrance, stopping within a short walk of every Springdale hotel and near several large visitor parking lots at the edge of town. During peak season, the last shuttle of the day leaves the Temple of Sinawava at 8:15pm.

## Getting Around

### Car

Zion Lodge guests may obtain a pass authorizing them to drive to the lodge, but in general, private vehicles are not allowed to drive up Zion Canyon Road during most of the year. You can drive to the campgrounds if you're staying there, and the road between the park entrance and the Zion-Mount Carmel Highway junction is open to all vehicles. In the off-season (Nov.-Feb.), private vehicles are allowed on all roads.

It's about 40 miles (64 km) from **Zion Canyon** to the **Kolob Canyons Visitor Center;** expect the drive to take about 45 minutes to an hour. In the winter, the Kolob Canyons Road may occasionally be closed by snow.

The drive from Zion Canyon to **Lava Point** on the Kolob Terrace Road takes about 1 hour 20 minutes to travel the 38 miles (61 km). The road is usually closed by snowfall from sometime in November until June.

From the **Zion Canyon Visitor Center** to the park's **east entrance** is less than 25 miles (40 km). Plan on taking at least 1 hour to make the drive. Even if you don't stop for hikes, the speed limit is 25-35 mph and there are lots of viewpoints along the way.

### Zion Canyon Shuttle

*7am-6:15pm Sat.-Sun. Feb.-early Mar., 7am-7:30pm daily early Mar.-mid May, 6am-8:15pm daily mid-May-Sept., 7am-6:30pm daily Oct.; seasonal hours vary year-to-year; no pets allowed; free*

The road through Zion Canyon is narrow with few pullouts, so to keep the road from becoming a parking lot, a shuttle bus provides regular free service through the canyon during most of the year. The bus line starts just inside the park entrance at the visitor center, and runs the length of Zion Canyon Road, stopping at scenic overlooks, trailheads, and Zion Lodge. Buses run frequently, but when the park is crowded, expect a wait.

Buses run as often as every seven minutes, but less frequently early in the morning, in the evening, and during the off season. When the park is at its most crowded, expect a wait. In the off-season, November-February, private vehicles are allowed on all roads, and the buses are out of service. Buses do include two mounts for bikes if you want to bike in and ride the shuttle back.

the hoodoo landscape of Bryce Amphitheater

# BRYCE CANYON NATIONAL PARK

A geologic fairyland of rock spires called hoodoos rises beneath the high cliffs of the Paunsaugunt Plateau. Eroded from soft limestone, Bryce's intricate maze glows red, orange, and pink, depending on the time of day and the weather.

Looking at hoodoos is like pondering clouds—a queen here, an elongated Russian doll there, or maybe a huddle of skyscrapers. According to the Paiute tale of the "Legend People," the hoodoos here are greedy humans frozen into stone for consuming too many resources.

Despite its name, Bryce Canyon isn't a canyon at all, but rather the largest of a series of massive amphitheaters cut into the Pink Cliffs. At Bryce Canyon National Park, you can gaze into the depths from viewpoints and trails along the rim or hike down moderately steep trails to wind your way through the spires.

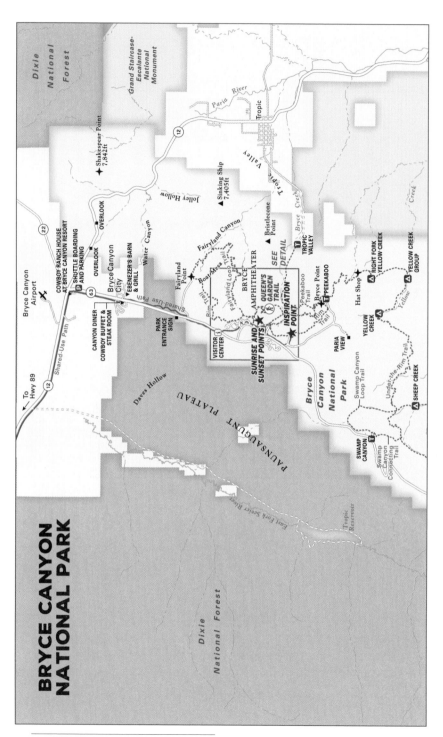

# BRYCE CANYON NATIONAL PARK

*Dixie National Forest*

Grand Staircase-Escalante National Monument

Paria River

Tropic

Shakespear Point 7,842ft

Jolley Hollow

Tropic Valley

Sinking Ship 7,405ft

Bryce Creek

Bristlecone Point

SEE DETAIL

Fairyland Canyon

Fairyland Point

Boat Mesa Trail

Fairyland Loop Trail

BRYCE AMPHITHEATER

QUEEN'S GARDEN TRAIL

INSPIRATION POINT

Peekaboo Trail

Bryce Point

PEEKABOO

Hat Shop

RIGHT FORK YELLOW CREEK

YELLOW CREEK GROUP

Rim Trail

Rim Trail

YELLOW CREEK

OVERLOOK

Bryce Canyon City

EBENEZER'S BARN & GRILL

Water Canyon

Fairyland Point

VISITOR CENTER

SUNRISE AND SUNSET POINTS

PARIA VIEW

Under-the-Rim Trail

SHEEP CREEK

COWBOY RANCH HOUSE AT BRYCE CANYON RESORT

SHUTTLE BOARDING AND PARKING

OVERLOOK

Bryce Canyon Airport

CANYON DINER
COWBOY BUFFET & STEAK ROOM

PARK ENTRANCE SIGN

Shared-Use Path

To Hwy 89

Daves Hollow

PAUNSAUGUNT PLATEAU

Bryce Canyon National Park

Swamp Canyon Loop Trail

SWAMP CANYON

Swamp Canyon Connecting Trail

East Fork Sevier River

Tropic Reservoir

*Dixie National Forest*

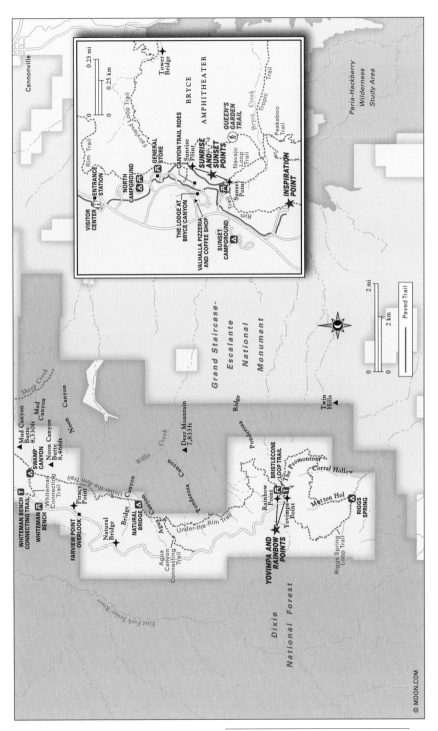

3

# TOP 3

★ **1. SUNRISE AND SUNSET POINTS:** At the namesake hours, these overlooks are irresistible, especially if you have a camera in hand (page 90).

★ **2. INSPIRATION POINT:** From Sunset Point, walk south along the Rim Trail to see a fantastic maze of hoodoos in the "Silent City." Many rows of narrow gullies here are more than 200 feet (61 m) deep (page 90).

★ **3. YOVIMPA AND RAINBOW POINTS:** The views from the scenic road's highest stop at 9,115 feet (2,778 m) are sweeping and spectacular (page 94).

# BRYCE CANYON 3 WAYS

## HALF DAY

For a quick visit to the park, focus your time on the short easy hikes along Bryce Amphitheater.

**1** Stop by the **Bryce Canyon Visitor Center** to take in the exhibits, watch the film, and if the timing is right, sign up for a ranger-led talk or activity. In high season, Geology Talks and guided Rim Walks are offered twice daily.

**2** Drive (or take the shuttle) to Sunset Point; from there, walk the **Rim Trail** to Sunrise Point. This portion of the Rim Trail is paved and mostly flat.

**3** From Sunrise Point, take **Queen's Garden Trail** down into the hoodoos. Follow the trail downhill among the pillars as far as you'd like, knowing that you'll need to climb back up to the rim.

**4** Drive (or take a shuttle) to **Inspiration Point** and gaze north over the maze of hoodoos in the "Silent City," while taking in the scale of Bryce Amphitheater.

**5** Stop for lunch or coffee at the **Lodge at Bryce Canyon,** a rustic yet classy log-and-stone structure built in 1924.

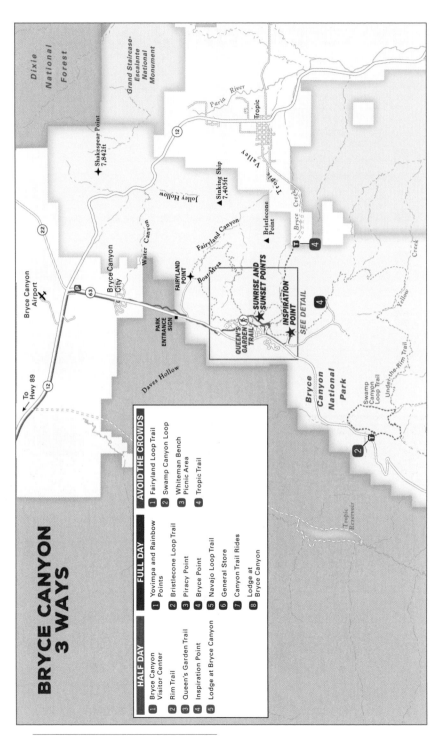

# BRYCE CANYON 3 WAYS

## HALF DAY
1. Bryce Canyon Visitor Center
2. Rim Trail
3. Queen's Garden Trail
4. Inspiration Point
5. Lodge at Bryce Canyon

## FULL DAY
1. Yovimpa and Rainbow Points
2. Bristlecone Loop Trail
3. Piracy Point
4. Bryce Point
5. Navajo Loop Trail
6. General Store
7. Canyon Trail Rides
8. Lodge at Bryce Canyon

## AVOID THE CROWDS
1. Fairyland Loop Trail
2. Swamp Canyon Loop
3. Whiteman Bench Picnic Area
4. Tropic Trail

Dixie National Forest

Grand Staircase-Escalante National Monument

Paria River

Tropic

★ Shakespear Point 7,842ft

Jolley Hollow

Water Canyon

▲ Sinking Ship 7,405ft

Tropic Valley

Bryce Creek

Fairyland Canyon

▲ Bristlecone Point

Bryce Canyon Airport ✈

Bryce Canyon City

FAIRYLAND POINT

Boat Mesa

SUNRISE AND SUNSET POINTS ★

★ INSPIRATION POINT

SEE DETAIL

QUEEN'S GARDEN TRAIL

PARK ENTRANCE SIGN

To Hwy 89

Daves Hollow

Bryce Canyon National Park

Yellow Creek

Creek

Under-the-Rim Trail

Swamp Canyon Loop Trail

Tropic Reservoir

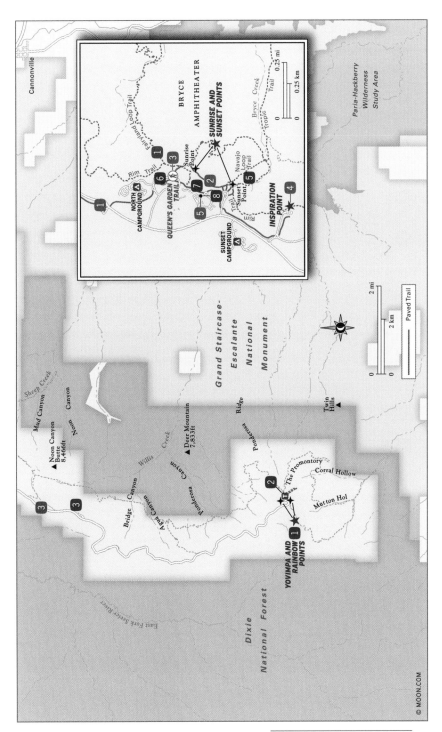

# FULL DAY

**1** Drive to the end of the park's scenic drive at **Yovimpa and Rainbow Points,** the highest area of the park (9,115 ft/2,778 m elevation).

**2** Walk the short **Bristlecone Loop Trail** to see small ancient bristlecone pines.

**3** On your way back down, turn off the main scenic drive toward two excellent viewpoints. First up: From Farview Point, take a short trail north to quieter **Piracy Point,** where the rock formations below resemble ships at sea.

**4** Your next viewpoint, **Bryce Point,** offers panoramas to the north, with the most expansive view over Bryce Amphitheater.

**5** Pull over at Sunset Point and put on your hiking boots. Follow **Navajo Loop Trail** down into the canyon to wander amid the hoodoos until you intersect with Queen's Garden Trail, which leads back up to the canyon's edge. This loop trail is 2.9 miles (4.6 km) long and will take 2-3 hours to hike.

**6** Break for a quick lunch at the **General Store** picnic area nearby. The store has sandwiches and other items if you didn't bring food with you.

**7** Take a two-hour horseback tour with **Canyon Trail Rides** (book online at least seven days in advance) that follows narrow trails to the base of the canyon and then back up to the rim, all accompanied by commentary on history and geology by your guide. Rides start at the horse corrals just north of the Lodge at Bryce Canyon.

**8** At this altitude, evenings are chilly even in summer. Relax and enjoy dinner by the fireplace at the historic **Lodge at Bryce Canyon.** If you still have energy after dinner, join rangers for evening programs at the lodge or in the North Campground, or watch the night sky through telescopes as part of a ranger-led dark-sky program at the visitor center.

# AVOID THE CROWDS

Because Bryce is shaped like a long string bean and is served by just one dead-end road, the farther south you go—away from the always busy Bryce Amphitheater area—the fewer crowds you'll encounter. To view and hike the amphitheater area without the crowds, get up early. Sunrise is a beautiful time to observe the hoodoos.

**1** Start your day at a quieter trail in the busy Bryce Amphitheater area: **Fairyland Loop Trail,** which is about 2 miles (3.2 km) north of the Sunrise Point crowds. From Fairyland Point trailhead, the loop back to the Rim Trail is a stout 8 miles (12.8 km), though many people hike down just far enough to see the "fairyland" of otherworldly hoodoos, then turn around and return up the same trail.

**2** Next up: another hiking trail. **Swamp Canyon Loop** drops down from Swamp Canyon trailhead to Under-the-Rim Trail along a pleasant seasonal stream. Connect back to the main highway along the Whiteman Connecting Trail.

**3** Pause for lunch at **Whiteman Bench Picnic Area**—a pleasant spot amid ponderosa pines and white firs.

**4** In the outskirts of the town of Tropic lies the only trail that begins in the amphitheater rather than the rim. From here, you can hike **Tropic Trail** up into the hoodoos and enjoy quite a bit of solitude in the process—until, that is, you intersect with Navajo Loop Trail.

## More Spots with Fewer Crowds

- Piracy Point (page 91)
- Bristlecone Loop Trail (page 103)

# BRYCE CANYON SCENIC DRIVE

**DRIVING DISTANCE:** 18 miles (29 km) one-way
**DRIVING TIME:** 35 minutes one-way, without stops
**START:** Park entrance
**END:** Rainbow Point

From elevations of about 8,000 feet (2,440 m) near the **visitor center,** the park's scenic drive gradually winds up 1,100 feet (335 m) to **Rainbow and Yovimpa Points.** About midway, ponderosa pines give way to spruce, fir, and aspen trees. On a clear day, you can enjoy vistas of more than 100 miles (161 km) from many viewpoints. Because of limited parking along the drive, trailers and RVs longer than 20 feet (6 m) must be left at the visitor center or your campsite. Visitors wishing to see all the viewpoints from Fairyland Point to Bryce Point can

walk on the Rim Trail, 5.5 miles (8.9 km) one-way.

Note that even though viewpoints are described here in north-to-south order, the stops are all on the east side of the drive, so rangers recommend driving all the way up to Rainbow Point, then visiting viewpoints on your way back down to avoid numerous lefthand turns across oncoming traffic. Of course, if you're just heading to one viewpoint or trailhead, it's fine to drive directly to it.

## FAIRYLAND POINT

The turnoff for Fairyland Point is just inside the park boundary, right before you get to the booth where payment is required; go north 0.8 mile (1.3 km) from the visitor center, then east 1 mile (1.6 km). Whimsical

Bryce Canyon in winter

rock formations line Fairyland Canyon a short distance below. You can descend into the area on the **Fairyland Loop Trail** or follow the **Rim Trail** for more views.

## ★ SUNRISE AND SUNSET POINTS

These overlooks are off to the left about 1 mile (1.6 km) south of the visitor center, and they're connected by a 0.5-mile (0.8-km) paved section of the **Rim Trail.** Panoramas from each point take in swaths of **Bryce Amphitheater** and beyond, including the Aquarius and Table Cliff Plateaus to the northeast, and the colorful cliffs rising 2,000 feet (610 m) or higher.

If you can, come early to Sunrise Point for a peaceful dawn viewing, or linger late at Sunset Point for a golden-hour hoodoo encounter. A short walk down either the **Queen's Garden Trail,** which begins at Sunrise

Point, or the **Navajo Loop Trail,** which starts at Sunset Point, will bring you closer to the **hoodoos,** making for a totally different experience than that found atop the rim.

## ★ INSPIRATION POINT

It's well worth the 0.75-mile (1.2-km) walk from Sunset Point south along the **Rim Trail** to see a fantastic maze of hoodoos in the **"Silent City"** from Inspiration Point, which actually consists of three viewpoint levels. The Lower and Mid viewpoints are also accessible by car via a spur road near the Bryce Point turnoff. Weathering along vertical joints has cut rows of narrow gullies, some more than 200 feet (61 m) deep. It's a short but steep 0.2-mile (0.3-km) walk to Upper Inspiration Point.

## BRYCE POINT

This overlook at the south end of

Fairyland Point (left); Sunset Point (right)

Bryce Amphitheater takes in expansive views to the north and east. It's also the start for the **Rim, Peekaboo Loop,** and **Under-the-Rim Trails.** From the turnoff 2 miles (3.2 km) south of the visitor center, follow signs 2.1 miles (3.4 km) in.

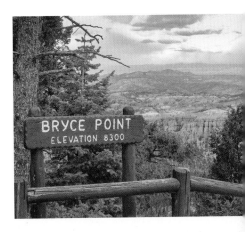

## PARIA VIEW

Cliffs drop precipitously into the headwaters of **Yellow Creek,** a tributary of the Paria River. Distant views take in the Paria River Canyon, White Cliffs (of Navajo sandstone), and Navajo Mountain. The rim of the park's plateau forms a drainage divide. Precipitation falling west of the rim flows gently into the East Fork of the Sevier River and the Great Basin; precipitation landing east of the rim rushes through deep canyons in the Pink Cliffs to the Paria River, then on to the Colorado River and the Grand Canyon. Take the turnoff for Bryce Point, then keep right at the fork.

## FARVIEW POINT

This sweeping panorama takes in a lot of geology. You'll see levels of the **Grand Staircase** that include the Aquarius and Table Cliff Plateaus to the northeast, Kaiparowits Plateau to the east, and White Cliffs to the southeast. Look beyond the White Cliffs to see a section of the Kaibab Plateau that forms the North Rim of the Grand Canyon. The overlook is on the left, 9 miles (14.5 km) south of the visitor center.

## PIRACY POINT

At this quieter overlook, you'll feel like you're in an airplane flying low over a busy shipyard. The buttes and hoodoos below strikingly resemble wooden pirate ships afloat in a sea of pines, especially if you squint.

Bryce Point (top); Paria View (middle); Farview Point (bottom)

sunrise in Bryce Canyon

Natural Bridge

high. Despite its name, this is an arch formed by weathering from rain and freezing, not by stream erosion, as with a true natural bridge. Once the opening reached ground level, runoff began to enlarge the hole and to dig a gully through it.

## ★ YOVIMPA AND RAINBOW POINTS

The land drops away in rugged canyons and fine views at the end of the scenic drive, 17 miles (27 km) south of the visitor center. At an elevation of 9,115 feet (2,778 m), this is the highest area of the park. Yovimpa and Rainbow Points are only a short walk apart yet offer different vistas. The **Bristlecone Loop Trail** is an easy 1-mile (1.6-km) loop from Rainbow Point to ancient bristlecone pines along the rim. The **Riggs Spring Loop Trail** makes a good day hike; you can begin from either Yovimpa Point or Rainbow Point and descend into canyons in the southern area of the park. The **Under-the-Rim Trail** starts from Rainbow Point and winds 23 miles (37 km) to Bryce Point; day hikers can make a 7.5-mile (12.1 km) trip by using the Agua Canyon Connecting Trail and a car shuttle.

Interestingly enough, this point overlooks a process called "stream piracy," where one stream of a river diverts water from another. The streams in question are Willis Creek, which is starting to divert water from Sheep Creek—both tributaries of the Paria River. From Farview Point, head north on a very short shaded trail to get here.

## NATURAL BRIDGE

This large feature lies just off the road to the east, 1.7 miles (2.7 km) past Farview Point. The span is 54 feet (16 m) wide and 95 feet (29 m)

Yovimpa Point (left); bare bristlecone pine trees along Bristlecone Loop Trail (right)

# BEST HIKES

## RIM TRAIL
**DISTANCE:** 11 miles (17.7 km) round-trip
**DURATION:** 5-7 hours round-trip
**ELEVATION GAIN:** 540 feet (165 m)
**EFFORT:** Easy
**TRAILHEADS:** Fairyland Point, Bryce Point
**SHUTTLE STOPS:** Fairyland Point, Bryce Point

Following the edge of Bryce Amphitheater, this trail involves minimal elevation change or technical terrain, but due to its length, falls somewhere between easy and moderate. Most people walk short sections of the rim in leisurely strolls or use the trail to connect with one of the five other trails that head down beneath the rim. Near the lodge, there's a 0.5-mile (0.8-km) stretch of trail between Sunrise and Sunset Points that is paved, nearly level, and wheelchair accessible; other parts are gently rolling.

## FAIRYLAND LOOP TRAIL
**DISTANCE:** 8 miles (12.9 km) round-trip
**DURATION:** 4-5 hours round-trip
**ELEVATION GAIN:** 2,300 feet (701 m)
**EFFORT:** Strenuous
**TRAILHEADS:** Fairyland Point, Sunrise Point
**SHUTTLE STOPS:** Fairyland Point, Sunrise Point

This trail winds in and out of colorful rock spires in the northern part of Bryce Amphitheater, a somewhat less visited area 1 mile (1.6 km) off the main park road. The most common trailhead is Fairyland Point, and you

can hike the loop in either direction, but counterclockwise is considered the easier option. You can also begin this loop hike at Sunrise Point, where you'll have to vie with more crowds in the first mile. Although the trail is well graded, remember that no matter which direction you hike this loop, there's a steep unrelenting climb at

Fairyland Loop Trail (top); Rim Trail (bottom)

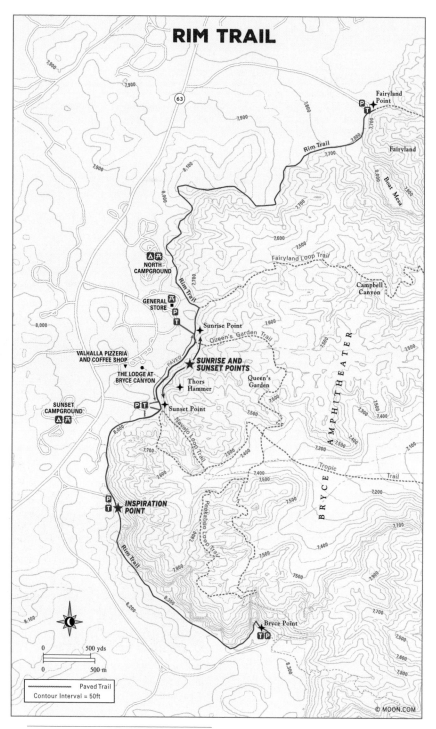

# RIM TRAIL

Fairyland Point

Fairyland

Boat Mesa

Rim Trail

Rim Trail

Fairyland Loop Trail

Campbell Canyon

NORTH CAMPGROUND

GENERAL STORE

Rim Trail

Sunrise Point

Queen's Garden Trail

**SUNRISE AND SUNSET POINTS**

VALHALLA PIZZERIA AND COFFEE SHOP

THE LODGE AT BRYCE CANYON

Thors Hammer

Queen's Garden

Sunset Point

Navajo Loop Trail

SUNSET CAMPGROUND

B R Y C E   A M P H I T H E A T E R

Tropic Trail

**INSPIRATION POINT**

Rim Trail

Peekaboo Loop Trail

Bryce Point

0    500 yds

0    500 m

Paved Trail
Contour Interval = 50ft

© MOON.COM

## FAIRYLAND LOOP TRAIL

the end to return to the rim. You can take a loop hike of 8 miles (12.9 km) from either Fairyland Point or Sunrise Point by using a section of the **Rim Trail;** a car shuttle between the two points saves 3 hiking miles (4.8 km). The whole loop is too long for many visitors, who enjoy short trips down and back to see this enchanting and quieter rock "fairyland."

## NAVAJO LOOP TRAIL

**DISTANCE:** 1.3 miles (2.1 km) round-trip
**DURATION:** 1.5 hours round-trip
**ELEVATION CHANGE:** 520 feet (158 m)
**EFFORT:** Moderate

**TRAILHEAD:** Sunset Point
**SHUTTLE STOP:** Sunset Point

From Sunset Point, this trail tours stunning hoodoo scenery as it drops 520 vertical feet (158 m) in 0.7 miles (1.2 km) through a narrow canyon. At the bottom, the loop leads into deep, dark **Wall Street**—an even narrower canyon 0.5 mile (0.8 km) long—before returning to the rim. Of all the trails in the park, this is the most prone to rockfall, so watch for slides or the sounds of falling rocks; it's not uncommon for at least part of the trail to be closed for rockfall. Other destinations from the bottom of Navajo Loop are **Twin Bridges,**

# TOP HIKE
## QUEEN'S GARDEN TRAIL

**DISTANCE:** 1.8 miles (2.9 km) round-trip
**DURATION:** 1.5 hours round-trip
**ELEVATION GAIN:** 320 feet (98 m)
**EFFORT:** Easy-moderate
**TRAILHEAD:** Sunrise Point
**SHUTTLE STOP:** Sunrise Point

This popular trail drops from Sunrise Point through impressive features in the middle of Bryce Amphitheater to a **hoodoo** resembling a portly Queen

Victoria. The easiest excursion below the rim, Queen's Garden also makes a good loop with **Navajo Loop** and **Rim Trails;** most people who do the loop prefer to descend the steeper Navajo Loop and climb out on Queen's Garden Trail for a 3.5-mile (5.6-km) hike.

hikers on Navajo Loop Trail

# BRISTLECONE PINE

bristlecone pine

Somewhere on earth, a bristlecone pine tree may be among the planet's oldest living organisms. The bristlecone pines here, while not the world's oldest, are up to 1,700 years old; there's one in California that's nearly 4,800 years old. These twisted, gnarly trees are easy to spot around **Rainbow Point** because they look their age.

What makes a bristlecone live so long? For one, its dense, resinous wood protects it from the insects, bacteria, and fungi that kill many other trees. It grows in a harsh dry climate where there's not a lot of competition from other plants. During droughts that would kill most plants, the bristlecone can slow its metabolism until it's practically dormant, then spring back to life when conditions improve. Although the dry desert air poses its own set of challenges, it also keeps the tree from rotting.

Besides its ancient look, a bristlecone pine can be recognized by its distinctive needles—they're packed tightly, five to a bunch, with the bunches running along the length of a branch, making it look like a bottle brush.

**Queen's Garden Trail, Peekaboo Loop Trail,** and **Tropic Trail.**

## PEEKABOO LOOP TRAIL

**DISTANCE:** 5.5 miles (8.9 km) round-trip
**DURATION:** 3-4 hours round-trip
**ELEVATION CHANGE:** 1,500 feet (457 m)
**EFFORT:** Moderate-strenuous

**TRAILHEAD:** Bryce Point
**SHUTTLE STOP:** Bryce Point

This enchanting walk is full of surprises at every turn—and there are lots of turns. The trail is in the southern part of Bryce Amphitheater, where many striking rock features await. The loop itself involves many ups and downs and a few tunnels. You can extend your hike by adding

# BRYCE CANYON FESTIVALS

Andromeda Galaxy seen from a telescope

Several festivals offer a chance to dig a little deeper into the park's astronomy, geology, and natural history. Although these are regular events, dates vary from year to year; check the park's website (www.nps.gov/brca) for the latest info.

If you want to delve into Bryce's geology, plan a trip in mid-July, when the free two-day **GeoFest** offers geologist-guided hikes and bus tours as well as evening programs, exhibits, and activities for kids. Check under Things To Do on the park's website for more information. Reserve seats on the bus tour in advance by calling 435/834-5290 and pick up tickets for guided hikes at the visitor center.

Bryce has been designated a Night Sky Sanctuary, and it's a great place to stargaze. Check the park's website for the date of the June **Astronomy Festival,** when you can explore stars, the planets, and the Milky Way in one of the darkest spots in the Lower 48. During the day, enjoy safe solar viewing through special telescopes at the visitor center, a workshop on telescope basics, and a star lab in the lodge auditorium. Evening talks prep visitors for stargazing through huge telescopes. Special shuttles run to the stargazing site; check at the visitor center or visit the park website for full schedules and shuttle details.

on **Navajo Loop** and **Queen's Garden Trail,** which connect with Peekaboo. This is the only trail in the park allowing equestrian use, and horseback riders have right of way; if possible, step to higher ground when you allow them to pass.

## SWAMP CANYON LOOP

**DISTANCE:** 4.3 miles (6.9 km) round-trip
**DURATION:** 2-3 hours round-trip
**ELEVATION CHANGE:** 800 feet (244 m)

**EFFORT:** Moderate
**TRAILHEAD:** Swamp Canyon
**SHUTTLE STOP:** Swamp Canyon

This loop comprises three trails: Swamp Canyon Connecting Trail, a short stretch of Under-the-Rim Trail, and Sheep Creek Connecting Trail. This hike takes you below the rim to a small sheltered canyon that is, by Utah standards, a wetland. Swamp Canyon's two tiny creeks and a spring provide enough moisture for lush grass and willows. Salamanders live here, as do a variety of birds; this is usually a good trail for bird-watching.

# BRISTLECONE LOOP TRAIL

**DISTANCE:** 1 mile (1.6 km) round-trip
**DURATION:** 30 minutes–1 hour round-trip
**ELEVATION CHANGE:** 195 feet (59 m)
**EFFORT:** Easy
**TRAILHEADS:** Rainbow Point, Yovimpa Point
**SHUTTLE STOP:** Rainbow Point

This easy 1-mile (1.6-km) loop begins from either Rainbow or Yovimpa Point and explores viewpoints and ancient bristlecone pines along the rim. These hardy trees survive fierce storms and extremes of hot and cold that no other tree can. Some of the bristlecone pines here are 1,700 years old.

Navajo Loop Trail

Under-the-Rim Trail (left); horseback riding in Bryce Canyon (right)

# BACKPACKING

Most trails in Bryce are best for day hikes, but the southern reaches of the park offer a couple of opportunities for overnight backpacking trips. All overnight camping trips require a backcountry **permit** ($5 per person per night).

The park's longest trail is the 23-mile (37-km) **Under-the-Rim Trail** that runs from Rainbow Point (at the end of the park's scenic drive) to Bryce Point. It's considered a fairly arduous trail, and for most hikers will require at least two days to complete. There are five backcountry campgrounds along the trail. Unless you want a 46-mile (74-km) round-trip adventure, you can just take the shuttle bus back to Rainbow Point. And if you don't want to commit to the entire trail, four different connector trails lead back to the rim and the scenic drive, making it possible to break this trek into shorter hikes.

Also departing from Rainbow Point, 8.5-mile (13.7-km) **Riggs Spring Loop Trail** is another strenuous hike with plenty of elevation change. With three campgrounds along the trail, it's usually considered a good overnight backpacking trip.

# HORSEBACK RIDING

### CANYON TRAIL RIDES
*Lodge at Bryce Canyon; 435/679-8665; www.canyonrides.com; Apr.-Oct.*

If you'd like to get down among the hoodoos, but aren't sure you'll have the energy to hike back up to the rim, consider letting a horse do the hard work. Canyon Trail Rides, a park concessionaire, offers two-hour ($75) and half-day ($100) guided rides near Sunrise Point. Both rides descend to the floor of the canyon; the longer ride follows the Peekaboo Loop Trail. Novices are welcome, but riders must be at least seven years old and weigh no more than 220 pounds.

## RUBY'S HORSEBACK ADVENTURES

*435/834-5341 or 866/782-0002; www.horserides.net; Apr.-Oct.*

Ruby's Horseback Adventures offers horseback riding in and near Bryce Canyon. There's a choice of half-day ($100) and full-day ($145, including lunch) trips, as well as a 1.5-hour trip ($75). During the summer, Ruby's also sponsors a rodeo (7pm Wed.-Sat., $15 adults, $10 ages 5-11) across from the inn.

# WINTER SPORTS

Although Bryce is most popular during the summer months (particularly Apr.-Oct.), it is beautiful and otherworldly in winter, when snow blankets the rock formations. Because Bryce is so high (elevation 8,000-9,000 ft/2,438-2,743 m), winter often lasts into April, but the main park roads and most viewpoints are plowed and open year-round.

## SNOWSHOEING AND CROSS-COUNTRY SKIING

Bryce has a great network of snowshoe and groomed cross-country ski trails. The Rim Trail is an excellent yet easy snowshoe or cross-country ski route. The roads to Paria View and Fairyland Point remain unplowed and are marked as **Paria Ski Trail** (a 5-mi/8.1-km loop) and **Fairyland Ski Trail** (a 2.5-mi/4-km loop) for snowshoers and cross-country skiers. Rent cross-country ski equipment just outside the park at Ruby's Inn (26 S. Main St.; 435/834-5341 or 866/866-6616; www.rubysinn.com).

The **Bryce Canyon Snowshoe Program** (435/834-4747; 2pm daily when possible; free) offers free snowshoes and poles when you join a guided hike with a snowshoe ranger. These 1-mile (1.6-km) outings are designed for beginners and depend on snow depth and ranger availability. On full-moon nights November-March, rangers add a moonlit snowshoe hike.

Although trail closures are relatively common due to rockfall or slick conditions, winter can be a fabulous time to get into the hoodoos. Crampons or simpler traction devices (such as Yaktrax) are often better than snowshoes for hiking steep trails with packed snow or ice.

## BRYCE CANYON NATIONAL PARK FOOD OPTIONS

| NAME | LOCATION | TYPE |
|------|----------|------|
| ★ Lodge at Bryce Canyon | Bryce Lodge | sit-down restaurant |
| General Store | Sunrise Point | takeout |
| Cowboy's Buffet and Steak Room | Ruby's Inn | sit-down restaurant |
| Canyon Diner | Ruby's Inn | quick meals and takeout |
| Ebenezer's Barn & Grill | Ruby's Inn | sit-down restaurant and entertainment |
| Cowboy Ranch House at Bryce Canyon Resort | Bryce Canyon Resort | sit-down restaurant and entertainment |

# FOOD

## LODGE AT BRYCE CANYON

*435/834-8700; www.*
*visitbrycecanyon.com; 7:30am-10am,*
*11:30am-3pm, and 5pm-9pm daily*
*Apr.-Oct.; $15-44*

The dining room at the Lodge at Bryce Canyon is classy and atmospheric, with a large stone fireplace and white tablecloths. The food is better than anything else you'll find in the area. For lunch ($10-15), the snack bar—which only has seating on an outdoor patio or in the lodge lobby—is a good bet in nice weather.

## BEST PICNIC SPOTS
### Sunset Point
*Shuttle stop: Sunset Point*

This popular picnic area is right along the Rim Trail, with easy access to parking and restrooms. As the name suggests, this viewpoint offers great vistas as the setting sun illuminates the hoodoos—an ideal spot for an evening picnic.

### General Store
*Shuttle stop: Sunrise Point*

If you didn't bring your own picnic fixings, you can get sandwiches and more on-the-go food at the General Store, then use the adjacent picnic

| FOOD | PRICE | HOURS |
|------|-------|-------|
| regional American | moderate | 7:30am-10am, 11:30am-3pm, and 5pm-9pm daily Apr.-Oct. |
| pizza and sandwiches | budget | 9am-6pm daily Apr.-Dec. |
| classic American | moderate | 6:30am-9:30pm daily summer, 6:30am-9pm daily winter |
| casual American | budget | 11:30am-8:30pm daily May-mid-Oct., 11:30am-7pm daily mid-Oct.-Apr. |
| cowboy-style food | moderate | 7pm dinner, 8pm show daily late Apr.-mid-Oct. |
| casual American | moderate | 7am-10pm daily |

area for alfresco dining. A restroom is also available.

## North Campground Picnic Area

*Shuttle Stop: Sunrise Point*

The park's North Campground also offers a picnic area not far from the Rim Trail and in a pleasant woodsy setting. Grills are available if you want to cook over a fire, and restrooms are a short stroll away.

## Whiteman Bench Picnic Area

*Shuttle Stop: Whiteman Bench*

If picnicking with the crowds around Bryce Amphitheater isn't for you, Whiteman Bench Picnic Area offers relative solitude 9.5 miles (15.2 km) south of the park entrance, along the scenic road toward Rainbow Point. The picnic area is also the trailhead for the Whiteman Connection Trail to the long-distance Under-the-Rim Trail.

## Rainbow Point

*Shuttle Stop: Rainbow Point*

At the southern terminus of the park's scenic drive, Rainbow Point Picnic Area is 18 miles (29 km) south of the park entrance. In addition to epic views, you'll find grills areas and restrooms.

## BRYCE CANYON NATIONAL PARK CAMPGROUNDS

| NAME | LOCATION | SEASON |
|------|----------|--------|
| **North Campground** | visitor center | at least one loop open year-round |
| **Sunset Campground** | across from Sunset Point | mid-Apr.-Oct. |

# CAMPING

The park's two campgrounds both have water and some pull-through spaces.

**Reservations** (877/444-6777; www.recreation.gov; May-Oct.) are accepted seasonally for Sunset Campground; North Campground is first come, first served. Make reservations at least two days in advance. Otherwise, try to arrive early for a space during the busy summer season—both campgrounds usually fill by 1pm or 2pm.

Basic groceries, camping supplies, coin-operated showers, and a laundry room are available at the General Store (mid-Apr.-late Sept.), between North Campground and Sunrise Point. During the rest of the year, you can go outside the park to Ruby's Inn for these services.

# LODGING

Travelers should book accommodations well in advance during peak season (Apr.-Oct.) in both the park and nearby areas. You'll also find significant variation in room prices from day to day and season to season. The rates cited below are generally for summer high season. What you may find online or by calling may differ markedly.

The Lodge at Bryce Canyon is the only hotel inside the park, and you'll generally need to make reservations months (even up to a year) in advance to get a room at this historic landmark (although it doesn't hurt to ask about last-minute vacancies). Other lodging is clustered near the park entrance road, but many do not offer much for the money. You'll find better accommodations in Tropic, 11 miles (17.7 km) east on Highway 12, and in Panguitch, 25 miles (40 km) northwest.

## LODGE AT BRYCE CANYON

*435/834-8700 or 877/386-4383; www.visitbrycecanyon.com; Apr.-Oct.; rooms $254-271, cabins $271*

Set among ponderosa pines a short walk from the rim, the Lodge at Bryce Canyon was built in 1923 by a division of the Union Pacific Railroad; a spur line once terminated at the front entrance. Listed in the National

| SITES AND AMENITIES | RV LIMIT | PRICE | RESERVATIONS |
|---|---|---|---|
| about 100 sites | 14 days; no max number of RVs | $20 tents, $30 RVs | yes (late May-mid-Oct.) |
| about 100 sites | 14 days; no max number of RVs | $20 tents, $30 RVs | yes (group site only) |

Register of Historic Places, this is the only lodging in the park itself, and it's heavy on charm. By far, this lodge has the best location of any Bryce-area accommodations. Options include suites in the lodge, motel-style guest rooms, and lodgepole pine cabins; all are clean and pleasant but fairly basic in terms of amenities. Reserving up to a year in advance is a good idea for the busy spring, summer, and early fall season.

Activities at the lodge include horseback rides, park tours, evening entertainment, and ranger talks. A gift shop sells souvenirs, while food can be found at both a restaurant and a snack bar.

Sunset Campground

## INFORMATION AND SERVICES

### Entrance Station

*$35 per vehicle, $30 motorcycles, $20 pp cyclists or pedestrians, admission good for 7 days and unlimited shuttle use*

From Highway 12, Highway 63 heads 3 miles (4.8 km) south to enter the park, where it becomes the main park road, going all the way south to Rainbow Point. This is the only way to enter the park; there are no other entrance stations.

### Visitor Center

*435/834-5322; 8am-8pm daily May-Sept., 8am-6pm daily mid-Mar.-Apr. and Oct., 8am-4:30pm daily Nov.-mid-Mar.*

From the turnoff on Highway 12, follow signs past Ruby's Inn for 4.5 miles (7.2 km) south to the park entrance; the visitor center is a short distance farther on the right. A 20-minute video, shown every half hour, introduces the park. Geologic exhibits illustrate how the land was formed and how it has changed. Historical displays cover the Paiute people, early nonnative explorers, and the first settlers alongside tree, flower, and wildlife IDs. Rangers present a variety of naturalist programs, including short hikes, mid-May-early September; schedules are posted at the visitor center.

## TRANSPORTATION

### Getting There

#### Car

Bryce Canyon National Park is just south of the incredibly scenic Highway 12, between Bryce Junction and Tropic. To reach the park from Bryce Junction (7 mi/11.3 km south of Panguitch at the intersection of U.S. 89 and Hwy. 12), head 14 miles (22.5 km) east on Highway 12, then south 3 miles (4.8 km) on Highway 63. From Escalante, it's about 50 miles (80 km) west on Highway 12 to the turnoff for Bryce; turn south onto Highway 63 for the final 3 miles (4.8 km) into the park (winter snows occasionally close this section). Both approaches have spectacular scenery.

#### From Zion National Park

Bryce Canyon National Park is 84 miles (135 km) from Zion. From Zion Canyon, head east via the Zion-Mount Carmel Highway (Hwy. 9); it's 24.5 miles (39 km) to its junction with U.S. 89. Turn north and follow U.S. 89 for 42 miles (68 km) to Bryce Junction. Turn east onto Highway 12 and travel 14 miles (22.5 km). Turn south on Highway 63; the entrance to Bryce Canyon National Park is 3 miles (4.8 km) down the road.

#### Parking

Free parking is available at the visitor center, at several viewpoints, and near

Ruby's Inn, outside the park entrance but near shuttle bus stops.

## Getting Around

### Car

You can drive your own vehicle into Bryce Canyon National Park. However, if you do drive into the park, don't plan to pull a trailer all the way to Rainbow Point: Trailers aren't allowed past Sunset Campground. Trailer parking is available at the visitor center.

Although all Bryce's main viewpoints and trailheads have parking lots, they can fill up by mid-morning. Note that tour buses roll in and out throughout much of the day, especially around Sunrise and Sunset Points. Although a fair number of visitors just sneak a peek and a selfie and return to their cars, taking the park shuttle lets you enjoy the hoodoos instead of worrying about traffic or parking.

Note that large RVs (any rig over 20 ft/6 m) are prohibited from parking in the Bryce Amphitheater (Sunrise, Sunset, Inspiration, Bryce, and Paria Viewpoints), as well as at the Lodge at Bryce Canyon and main visitor center lot, during shuttle hours. They also can't drive the park road beyond the turnoff to Inspiration, Bryce, and Paria Viewpoints. Plan to park at the Additional Parking Lot across from the visitor center, the Shuttle Station parking lot across from Ruby's Inn, or your campsite, and use the park shuttle to get around.

### Bryce Canyon Shuttle

*every 15-20 minutes 8am-8pm daily mid-Apr.-mid-Oct., shorter hours early and late in season; free*

During the summer, Bryce hosts an enormous number of visitors. To keep the one main road along the rim from turning into a parking lot, the National Park Service runs the Bryce Canyon Shuttle. Buses run during the peak summer season from the shuttle parking and boarding area at the intersection of Highways 12 and 63 to the visitor center, with stops at Ruby's Inn and Ruby's Campground. From the visitor center, the shuttle travels to the park's developed areas, including all the main amphitheater viewpoints, Sunset Campground, and the Lodge at Bryce Canyon. Passengers can take as long as they like at any viewpoint, then catch a later bus. The shuttle bus service also makes it easier for hikers, who don't need to worry about car shuttles between trailheads.

Use of the shuttle bus system is included in the cost of admission to the park, but it is not mandatory; you can still drive your own vehicle. However, park officials note that there is generally one parking space for every four cars entering Bryce.

Bryce Canyon hoodoos

# GEOLOGY

At any of Utah's national parks, the first things you'll probably notice are rocks. Vegetation is sparse and soil is thin, so the geology steals the show. Particularly stunning views await in deep canyons carved through the layers by rivers. Hoodoos, arches, and other odd features formed through the erosion of the giant geologic layer cake that is the Colorado Plateau.

# HOODOOS

Hoodoos are thin spires or columns of stone that have eroded from layers of colorful sedimentary deposits. The hoodoos of Bryce stand in rows of straight alignment, giving the impression of marching soldiers, or the remnants of ancient temples. Although many visitors assume that wind shaped these hoodoos, they were, in fact, formed by water, ice, and gravity, interacting on rocks of varying hardness over millions of years.

When the Colorado Plateau uplifted, vertical breaks—called joints—formed in the plateau. Joints allowed water to flow into the rock. As water flowed through these joints, erosion widened them into rivulets, gullies, and eventually deep slot canyons. Even more powerful than water, the action of ice freezing, melting, then freezing again, as it does about 200 days a year at Bryce, causes ice wedges to form within the rock joints, eventually breaking the rock.

The massive amphitheater that is Bryce is composed of limestone, siltstone, dolomite, and mudstone layers. Each rock type erodes at a different rate, carving the strange shapes found here.

Like the word "voodoo," "hoodoo" is sometimes used to describe religious beliefs and practices. Early Spanish explorers transferred the mystical sense of the word to these rock formations because they believed that Native Americans worshipped these "enchanted rocks." Yet while early indigenous people considered many hoodoo areas sacred, there is no evidence that they worshipped the stones themselves.

## WHERE TO SEE HOODOOS

- Bryce Point (page 90)

- Inspiration Point (page 90)

- Queen's Garden Trail (page 98)

- Riggs Spring Loop (page 94)

- Rim Trail (page 95)

- Zion-Mount Carmel Highway (page 55)

hoodoos from Bryce Point (left); hoodoos along Queen's Garden Trail (right)

## ZION'S ROCK FORMATIONS

What Zion lacks in hoodoos, it makes up for in other distinctive rock formations:

### THE PATRIARCHS

Views of these three sandstone peaks (named Abraham, Isaac, and Jacob) are accessible via a short trail from the **Court of the Patriarchs Viewpoint** in Zion National Park (page 51).

### GREAT WHITE THRONE

A chunk of Navajo sandstone that (along with the Patriarchs) is emblematic of Zion. It's visible from various points along **Zion Canyon Scenic Drive,** and particularly lovely at sunset (page 55).

Checkerboard Mesa

### CHECKERBOARD MESA

This hulking rock's distinctive pattern was caused by a combination of vertical fractures and horizontal bedding planes, both accentuated by weathering. View it as you drive from Zion toward Bryce along **Zion-Mount Carmel Highway** (page 57).

# ARCHES

Although Zion and Bryce aren't known for their rock arches (unlike southeast Utah's Arches National Park), they can be found in both parks.

Aches form as a result of an unusual combination of geologic forces. About 300 million years ago, evaporation of inland seas left behind a salt layer over 3,000 feet (915 m) thick in southern Utah's Paradox Basin. Sediments, including those that later became the arches, then covered the salt. Unequal pressures caused the salt to gradually flow upward in places, bending the overlying sediments. These upfolds, or anticlines, later collapsed when groundwater dissolved the underlying salt.

The faults and joints caused by the uplift and collapse opened the way for erosion to carve freestanding rock fins. The fins' uniform strength and hard upper surfaces are ideal for arch formation. Freeze-thaw cycles and exfoliation (flaking caused by expansion when water or frost penetrates rock) continued to peel away the softer rock until holes formed in

The Narrows

Natural Bridge

A number of terms are used to describe rock arches. Although the term "windows" often refers to openings in large walls of rock, windows and arches are really the same. Arches are also sometimes referred to as natural bridges, but geologically speaking, bridges have live streams running through them, while arches do not.

## WHERE TO SEE ARCHES

some fins. Rockfall within the holes enlarged the arches.

- Canyon Overlook Trail (page 67)
- Kolob Arch (page 58)
- Natural Bridge (page 94)

# COLORFUL ROCKS

In Utah, you'll get used to seeing a lot of colorful rock formations. Color gives you clues to the composition and geologic history of the rock. In general:

**Red rocks** are stained by rusty iron-rich sediments washed down from mountains, and they are a clue that erosion has occurred.

**Gray or brown rocks** were deposited by ancient seas.

**White rocks** are colored by their "glue," the limey remains of dissolved seashells that leach down and harden sandstone.

**Black rocks** are volcanic in origin, though not all volcanic, or igneous, rocks are black. Igneous rocks are present in the La Sal and Abajo Mountains. These mountains are "laccoliths," formed by molten magma that pushed through the sedimentary layers, leaking deeper into some layers than others and eventually forming broad dome-shaped

protuberances, which were eroded into soft peaks, then carved by glaciers into the sharp peaks we see today.

A layer of lava also caps the Paunsaugunt, Markagunt, and Aquarius Plateaus, which have lifted above the main level of the Colorado Plateau. This mostly basalt layer was laid down about 37 million years ago, before the Colorado Plateau began to uplift.

And what about those dark-colored vertical stripes you often see on sandstone cliff faces across the Colorado Plateau? **Desert varnish** is mostly composed of very fine clay particles, rich in iron and manganese. It's not entirely known how these streaks form, but it seems likely that they're at least partly created by mineral-rich water coursing down the cliffs, followed by wind-blown clay dust sticking to these wet areas. Bacteria and fungi on the rock surface may help this process along by absorbing manganese and iron from the atmosphere and precipitating it as a black layer of manganese oxide or reddish iron oxide. The clay particles in this thin layer of varnish help shield the bacteria against the drying effects of the desert sun. Prehistoric rock artists worked with desert varnish, chipping away the dark surface to expose the lighter underlying rocks.

## WHERE TO SEE COLORFUL ROCKS

- **Red Rocks:** Altar of Sacrifice (page 51)
- **Gray or Brown Rocks:** Grand Staircase (page 91)
- **White Rocks:** Great White Throne (page 55), Checkerboard Mesa (page 57)

Great White Throne

- **Pink Rocks:** Hoodoos in Bryce Amphitheater (page 90)
- **Desert Varnish:** Zion Canyon (page 49), Kolob Canyons (page 57)

# CANYONS

Though much of southwest Utah is arid and desertlike, streams and rivers have worked for millions of years to carve deep canyons in the underlying sandstone and limestone. Because there's little vegetation on the canyon walls, it's easy to see the many layers of sandstone and marine sediments that make up the area's bedrock. By the way, even though it's called Bryce Canyon, the main feature in that park is actually not a canyon, but a vast eroded amphitheater filled with multicolored hoodoos.

## WHERE TO SEE CANYONS

- Hidden Canyon Trail (page 61)
- The Narrows (page 64)
- Navajo Loop Trail (page 97)

bighorn sheep in Zion

# FLORA & FAUNA

Several different life zones exist across the Colorado Plateau. In the low desert, shrubs eke out a meager existence. Climb higher and you'll pass through grasslands, sage, and piñon-juniper woodlands leading to ponderosa pine. Of all these zones, the piñon-juniper is most common.

But it's not a lockstep progression of plant A at elevation X to plant B at elevation Z. Soils are an important consideration, and Utah's many microenvironments can lead to surprising plant discoveries. See what plants you find in these different habitats:

- **Slickrock:** Cracks in the rock can gather enough soil to host a little life.

- **Riparian:** Moist areas with the greatest diversity.

- **Terraces and open space:** Areas between riverbank and slickrock, where shrubs dominate.

With more than 800 native species, Zion has the greatest plant diversity of any of the Utah parks. Although they're not thought of as great "wildlife parks" like Yellowstone or Denali, Utah's national parks are home to plenty of animals. Desert animals are often nocturnal and unseen by park visitors.

# HOW PLANTS SURVIVE IN THE DESERT

Most of the plants in Utah's national parks are well adapted to desert life. Many are succulents like cacti, which have their own water storage systems in fleshy stems or leaves. Succulents swell with stored moisture in spring, then slowly shrink and wrinkle as they use up their reserves.

Other plants have different strategies for making the most of scarce water. Some, like yuccas, have deep roots, taking advantage of any moisture in the soil. The leaves of desert plants are often spiny, exposing less surface area to the sun. Leaves may have very small pores to slow transpiration, or stems coated with a resinous substance, which also decelerates water loss. Hairy or light-colored leaves help reflect sunlight.

Most desert wildflowers are annuals. They bloom in the spring when water is available, form seeds that can survive the hot summer, then die. A particularly wet spring means a bumper crop of wildflowers.

Even though mosses aren't usually thought of as desert plants, they grow in seeps along canyon walls and in cryptobiotic soils. When water is unavailable, mosses dry up, only to plump up again when water returns.

Junipers have a fairly drastic way of dealing with water shortage: self-pruning. During a prolonged dry spell, a juniper tree can shut off the flow of water to one or more of its branches, sacrificing selected limbs to keep itself alive.

lavender leaf primrose (top); datura stramonium (bottom)

# MORMON TEA

Mormon tea

It's not the showiest wildflower in the desert, but Mormon tea *(Ephedra viridis)* is widespread across southern Utah. This broom-like plant is remarkably well adapted to aridity. Its branches contain chlorophyll and can conduct photosynthesis, while its small scale-like leaves reduce the amount of moisture lost to transpiration.

Mormon tea has long been popular among desert-dwelling humans. Native Americans used this plant medicinally as a tea for stomach and bowel disorders as well as for colds, fever, and headaches. Some used it to control bleeding and as a poultice for burns.

All parts of the plant contain a small amount of ephedrine, a stimulant that in large concentrations can be quite harmful. The Latter-day Saint pioneers of southern Utah are forbidden from drinking coffee or other stimulants, so when they learned that the boiled stems of *Ephedra viridis* gave them a mild lift, they approached Brigham Young, the head of the Latter-day Saints. Young gave the tea his stamp of approval, and the plant's common name grew out of its widespread use by Latter-day Saints.

The tea itself is yellowish and not exactly tasty. To increase the tea's palatability, it's often mixed with mint, lemon, and sugar or honey. Pioneers liked to add strawberry jam to their Mormon tea. If you're tempted to try a cup, don't harvest plants in a national park. People who are pregnant or nursing and anyone with high blood pressure, heart disease, diabetes, or other health issues should avoid even the small amounts of ephedrine present in Mormon tea.

## CRYPTOBIOTIC SOIL

Across much of the Colorado Plateau, the soil is alive. What looks like a blackish-brown crust is actually a dense network of blue-green algae intertwined with soil particles, lichens, moss, green algae, and microfungi. This slightly sticky, crusty mass holds the soil together, slowing erosion. Its sponge-like consistency allows it to soak up and retain water, reducing runoff and evaporation.

This biological soil plays a critical role in the resilience of desert ecosystems. Plants growing in cryptobiotic soil have a great advantage over plants rooted in dry sandy soil. In addition to retaining moisture, cryptobiotic soil helps prevent erosion from wind and water.

The upshot? Watch where you step. Cryptobiotic soils can take centuries to fully develop and are extremely fragile. Make every effort to avoid treading on this incredible desert resource by sticking to trails, slickrock, or rocks.

# HANGING GARDENS

Along Zion's Virgin River canyon, look for maidenhair ferns, mosses, shooting stars, monkey flowers, columbine, orchids, and bluebells springing from the cliff walls. These improbably lush pockets of plant life are called "hanging gardens."

Hanging gardens take advantage of a unique microclimate created by the meeting of two rock layers: Navajo sandstone and Kayenta shale. Water percolates down through porous sandstone. When the water hits the denser shale layer, it travels laterally over the harder rock, emerging at cliff's edge and supporting the gardens.

Although spring and early summer are peak times for wildflower blooms, the trickles of water keep these plants looking pretty good even in summer's heat.

## WHERE TO SEE HANGING GARDENS

- Emerald Pools Trails (page 62)
- Riverside Walk (page 64)
- Temple of Sinawava (page 53)
- Weeping Rock Trail (page 59)

# SMALL MAMMALS

Most squirrels, packrats, kangaroo rats, chipmunks, and porcupines spend their days in burrows. One of the few desert rodents that forages by day across lower elevations is the white-tailed antelope squirrel, which resembles a chipmunk. Its white tail reflects sunlight, and when it needs to cool down, it smears its face with saliva. Higher up at Bryce's

hanging gardens alongside the Riverside Walk

chipmunk (left); grey fox (right)

elevations, for example, you'll see golden-mantled ground squirrels.

Look for rabbits—desert cottontails and jackrabbits—at dawn and dusk.

Kangaroo rats are particularly skilled at desert life. They spend their days in cool burrows, eat only plants, and never drink water. Instead, a kangaroo rat metabolizes dry food in a way that produces water.

Utah prairie dogs have been given a new lease on life in Bryce National Park. In 1973, the animals were listed as an endangered species and reintroduced to Bryce. Today, nearly 200 of them live in the park. Prairie dogs live together in social groups called colonies or towns, which are laced with burrows that feature a network of entrances for popping in and out of the ground. Prairie dogs are prey to badgers, coyotes, hawks, and snakes, so a colony will post lookouts. Under threat, the lookouts "bark" to warn the colony. Utah prairie dogs hibernate during winter and emerge from their burrows to mate furiously in early April.

Porcupines are common in Zion. Although they prefer to live in forested areas, especially the piñon-juniper zone, they sometimes forage in streamside brush. These nocturnal creatures have also been known to visit campsites, where they like to gnaw on sweaty boots or backpack straps.

## WHERE TO SEE SMALL MAMMALS

- Riverside Walk (page 64)

- Picnic areas—but don't feed these furry friends (pages 72 and 106)

# LARGE MAMMALS

Mule deer are common across Utah, as are coyotes. Other large mammals include bighorn sheep and predators like mountain lions, black bears, and coyotes—sightings are rare. If you're lucky, you'll get a glimpse of a bobcat or a fox.

If you're hiking in Bryce early in the morning and see something that looks like a small dog in a tree, it's probably a grey fox. These small (5-10 pounds) foxes live in forested areas and can climb trees. They're most commonly spied on the

# MOUNTAIN LION ENCOUNTERS

mountain lion

Imagine hiking down a trail and suddenly noticing fresh large paw prints. Mountain lion or Labrador retriever? Here's how to tell the difference: Mountain lions usually retract their claws when they walk. Dogs, of course, can't do this. So if close inspection reveals toenails, it's most likely a canine's paw.

While mountain lions range through Zion and Bryce, sightings are rare—though incidents of mountain lion-human confrontations have recently increased and received much publicity. The increase may be due to the growth of the cougar population and drought pushing deer (i.e., their dinner) closer to urban areas. These ambush hunters usually prey on sick or weak animals, but will occasionally attack people, especially children and small adults. In mountain lion territory—most of southern Utah—keep your kids close.

That said, mountain lion attacks are extremely rare, with only a handful reported in the past few decades. The risk in Utah is also lower than in other mountain lion habitats. For example, the state sees fewer incidents and attacks than Colorado, California, and British Columbia.

If you're stalked by a mountain lion, make yourself look big by raising your arms, waving a big stick, or spreading your coat. Maintain direct eye contact with the animal, and do not turn your back to it. If the mountain lion begins to approach, throw rocks and sticks, and continue to look large and menacing while slowly backing away. In the case of an attack, fight back—do not "play dead."

connecting trail between the Queen's Garden and Navajo Loop Trails.

Desert bighorns have been reintroduced in Zion and can occasionally be spotted in steep rocky areas on the park's east side.

## WHERE TO SEE LARGE MAMMALS

- Navajo Loop and Queen's Garden Trail (pages 97 & 98)
- Zion-Mount Carmel Highway (page 55)

# REPTILES

Reptiles thrive in the desert. As cold-blooded, or ectothermic, animals, their body temperature depends on the environment, rather than on internal metabolism, and it's easy for them to keep warm in the heat. In the cold, reptiles hibernate or drastically slow their metabolism.

Zion is home to a number of lizards. Several (all female) species of parthenogenetic lizards reproduce by laying eggs that are clones of themselves. Several species of snakes, including rattlesnakes, also live here, but given a chance, they'll get out of your way rather than

strike—still, it's a good reason to wear sturdy boots. And you're unlikely to see them, but Zion is also home to desert tortoises as well.

Bryce also has a few lizards and snakes—including great basin rattlesnakes—but fewer reptiles due to its higher elevations and cooler temperatures.

## WHERE TO SEE REPTILES

- Kayenta Trail (page 62)
- Taylor Creek Trail (page 68)

plateau fence lizard

# AMPHIBIANS

Although they're not usually thought of as desert animals, a variety of frogs and toads live on the Colorado Plateau. While none call the higher reaches of Bryce home, six species of frogs and toads—as well as the tiger salamander—reside in the Zion area near the Virgin River. Tadpoles live in wet springtime potholes as well as in streams and seeps. If you're camping in a canyon, you may be lucky enough to be serenaded by a toad chorus.

The big round toes of the small spotted canyon tree frog make it easy to identify—that is, if you can see this well-camouflaged amphibian in the first place. They're most active at night, spending their days on streamside rocks or trees.

Other frogs present in Zion include the northern leopard frog and the red spotted toad.

## WHERE TO SEE AMPHIBIANS

- Emerald Pools Trails (page 62)

- Along the Virgin River (pages 58 and 64)

# BIRDS

Have you ever seen a bird pant? This is actually how desert birds expel heat. They also allow heat to escape by drooping their wings away from their bodies and exposing thinly feathered areas.

The various habitats across the Colorado Plateau, such as piñon-juniper, perennial streams, dry washes, and rock cliffs, allow hundreds of species of birds to find permanent and temporary homes along migration routes.

Birders will find over 200 species in each park, with the greatest variety of species near rivers and streams. Other birds, such as golden eagles, kestrels (small falcons), and peregrine falcons, nest high on cliffs and patrol open areas for prey. Commonly seen hawks include the red-tailed and northern harrier. Late-evening strollers may see great horned owls, and in Zion, you can find the Mexican spotted owl. California condors were reintroduced to Zion in 1996 and can now be seen at Lava Point, Canyon Overlook, and Angels Landing.

People usually detect the canyon wren by its lovely song. This small long-beaked bird nests in cavities along cliff faces. The related rock wren is—as its name implies—a rock collector: It paves a trail to

American dipper

its nest with pebbles, and the nest itself is lined with rocks. Another canyon bird, the white-throated swift, swoops and calls as it dramatically chases insects and mates in flight. Swifts are often seen near violet-green swallows, which are equally gymnastic fliers.

Several species of hummingbird (mostly black-chinned, but also broad-tailed and rufous) are often seen in both parks in summer. Woodpeckers are also common, including the northern flicker and red-naped sapsucker, and flycatchers like Say's phoebe, western kingbird, and western wood-pewee can be spotted too. Two warblers—the yellow and the yellow-rumped—are common in summer, and Wilson's warbler stops by during spring and fall migrations. Horned larks are present year-round.

Mountain bluebirds are colorful, making them easy for a novice to identify. Look for the American dipper along the Virgin River in Zion. This small gray bird distinguishes itself from other similar birds by its habit of plunging headfirst into the water in search of insects.

Other icons of Western avian life—the turkey vulture, the raven, and the magpie—are widespread and easily spotted.

## WHERE TO SEE BIRDS

- Canyon Overlook Trail (page 67)
- Kolob Terrace Road (page 53)
- Tropic Trail (page 101)

black-chinned hummingbird

# FISH

Obviously, deserts aren't particularly known for their aquatic life, and the big rivers of the Colorado Plateau are now dominated by nonnative species such as channel catfish and carp. Many of these fish were introduced as game fish. While you won't find any fish among the hoodoos of Bryce, Zion has some of these nonnative species in the Virgin River, along with some native species, including the Virgin spinedace and the desert sucker.

# SPIDERS AND SCORPIONS

Tarantulas, black widows, and scorpions all inhabit the Colorado Plateau. Although the black widow spider's venom is toxic, tarantulas deliver only a mildly toxic bite (and they rarely bite humans). A scorpion's sting is similar to a bee's, and most people don't have a very severe reaction. You'll find these insects in Zion, but only butterflies and far less threatening critters in Bryce.

Tarantulas hang out in underground burrows, or occasionally on trails or roads. You'll see other spiders on their webs low to the ground, in shaded rock corners or crevices, and high up on cliff walls. Scorpions usually like to hide. You'll find them in valleys and washes, usually under logs or rocks. Scorpions and most spiders are nocturnal, so you're unlikely to see them active during the day.

tarantula

The Narrows

ESSENTIALS

# GETTING THERE

## AIR

Many visits to Utah's national parks begin in Salt Lake City. Its busy airport and plethora of hotels make it an easy place to begin and end a trip. However, it's smart to consider flying into Harry Reid International Airport in Las Vegas instead. Not only is it closer to Zion and Bryce, but car rentals are usually about $100 cheaper per week.

Although it may not seem intuitive to start your tour of Utah's national parks in Denver, this works well for many folks, especially those who fly from European cities to Denver International Airport. From there, it's easy to rent a car or RV and begin a scenic road trip that typically includes Rocky Mountain National Park, Utah's five national parks, and the Grand Canyon before terminating in Las Vegas.

### Salt Lake City International Airport

SLC; 776 N. Terminal Dr.; 801/575-2400; www.slcairport.com
**DRIVING TIME TO ZION:** 4.5 hours, mostly along I-15 south
**DRIVING TIME TO BRYCE:** 4 hours, mostly along I-15 south

### Harry Reid International Airport (Las Vegas)

LAS; 5757 Wayne Newton Blvd.; 702/261-5743; www.mccarran.com
**DRIVING TIME TO ZION:** 3 hours, mostly along I-15 north
**DRIVING TIME TO BRYCE:** 4 hours, mostly along I-15 north

### Denver International Airport

DEN; 8500 Peña Blvd.; 303/342-2000; www.flydenver.com
**DRIVING TIME TO ZION:** 10.5 hours, mostly along I-70 west
**DRIVING TIME TO BRYCE:** 9.5 hours, mostly along I-70 west

## BUS

**Greyhound** buses stop in **Salt Lake City** (160 W. South Temple St.; 801/355-9579 or 800/231-2222; www.greyhound.com) and Las Vegas (6675 Gilespie St.; 702/383-9792; www.greyhound.com). Buses generally run north and south along I-15 and east and west along I-80. However, you won't be able to take the bus to any of Utah's national parks, so at some point, you'll need to rent a car.

## CAR

To get to Zion and Bryce from Salt Lake City, simply take I-15 south; drive time is about 4.5 hours.

From Las Vegas, it's just 120 miles (193 km) northeast on I-15 to St. George, with Zion just 43 miles (69 km) farther. From Denver, follow I-70 west, up over the Continental Divide along the Rocky Mountains, and down to the Colorado River.

# GETTING AROUND

Aside from ambitious bikepackers and hitchhikers, getting around southern Utah requires using some form of automobile. Public transportation is nonexistent between the parks, distances are great, and roads are often circuitous since they must circumnavigate geographical obstacles. Cars are easily rented in gateway cities, including Salt Lake City, Las Vegas, and Denver.

## TRAVELING BY RV

Traveling the Southwest in an RV is a time-honored tradition, and travelers will have no problem finding RV or van rentals in nearby major cities. The parks have good campgrounds, and towns like Springdale have spiffy campground options with extras like swimming pools and fine-dining cookouts.

Note that some parks limit RV access. During high season, no vehicles are allowed in Zion, and visitors must ride the shuttle bus along Zion Canyon Road. In Bryce, vehicles measuring 20 feet (6 m) or longer are restricted from Bryce Amphitheater area during shuttle hours.

## FAST FACTS

### ZION

- Inaugurated: 1919; Kolob Canyons added 1956
- Visitation in 2022: 4.7 million
- Area: 229 square miles (593 sq km)

### BRYCE

- Inaugurated: 1928; designated a national monument 1923
- Visitation in 2022: 2.3 million
- Area: 56 square miles (145 sq km)

## DRIVING THE PARKS

From late spring through early fall, patience is the key to enjoying your drive in and around Utah's national parks. Roads are often crowded with slow-moving RVs, and traffic jams are not uncommon.

If you're traveling on back roads, make sure you have plenty of gas, even if it means paying top dollar at a small-town gas pump (this will often be your only option).

Summer heat in the desert puts an extra strain on both cars and drivers. It's worth double-checking your vehicle's cooling system, engine oil, transmission fluid, fan belts, and tires to ensure they're in good condition. Carry several gallons of water in case of a breakdown or radiator trouble. Never leave children or pets in a parked car during warm weather—temperatures inside can cause fatal heatstroke in minutes.

In late summer, storms frequently flood low spots in the road. Wait for the water level to subside before crossing. Dust storms can completely block visibility but tend to be short-lived. During such storms, pull completely off the road, stop, and turn off your lights so as not to confuse other drivers. Radio stations carry frequent weather updates when weather hazards emerge.

If stranded, stay with your vehicle unless you know for sure where to go for help. Leave a note on your vehicle explaining your route and departure time. Airplanes can easily spot a stranded car (tie a piece of cloth to your antenna), but a person walking is more difficult to see. It's best to carry emergency supplies: blankets or sleeping bags, a first-aid kit, tools, jumper cables, a shovel, traction mats or chains, a flashlight, rain gear, water, food, and a can opener.

### Maps

The Utah Department of Transportation prints and distributes a free, regularly updated map of Utah. Ask for it when you call for information or when you stop at a visitor information office. Benchmark Maps' *Utah Road and Recreation Atlas* is loaded with beautiful maps, recreation information, and global positioning system (GPS) grids. If you're planning on extensive backcountry exploration, be sure to ask locally about conditions.

If you're looking for USGS topo maps, download them for free at www. topozone.com.

### Off-Road Driving

Here are some tips for safely traversing the backcountry in a vehicle (preferably one with four-wheel drive, high clearance, and tires with good traction):

- Drive slowly enough to choose a safe path and avoid obstacles such as rocks or giant potholes, but keep up enough speed to propel yourself through sand or mud.

- If it has recently rained or it starts to rain, consider turning back. Moderate or heavy rainfall can quickly turn dirt roads into tire-sucking mud

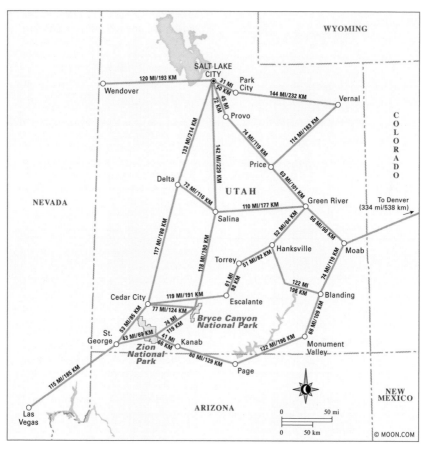

that could leave you stranded in the backcountry. Check with a visitor center for road conditions and forecasts beforehand.

- Keep an eye on the route ahead of you. If there are significant obstacles, get out of your vehicle and survey the situation.

- Reduce the tire pressure if you're driving across long stretches of sand.

- Drive directly up or down the fall line of a slope. Cutting across diagonally may seem less frightening, but it puts you in a position to slide or roll over.

If you really want to learn to drive a 4WD rig, consider signing up for a class.

## Charging Your Electric Car

Electric vehicle (EV) charging stations are present in some areas of southern Utah, but if you plan to explore far-flung destinations, a little preplanning is in order. At press time, EV charging stations are available at St. George, Cedar City, Springdale, the visitor center at Zion National Park, Ruby's Inn (near Bryce Canyon National Park), Green River, St. George, Kanab, Boulder (at Boulder Mountain Lodge), Moab, Blanding, and Page, Arizona. That leaves big areas of southern Utah with no EV charging services, so plan your route and charging schedule ahead of time.

## SHUTTLES

Both Zion and Bryce Canyon National Parks offer free shuttle bus service during peak seasons along their primary roads to reduce traffic and vehicular impact on the parks. In Zion, shuttles pick up visitors at various points around the nearby town of Springdale and take them to the park gate, where another shuttle runs visitors up Zion Canyon Road, stopping at trailheads, scenic overlooks, and Zion Lodge. Essentially, during peak season, private cars are no longer allowed on Zion Canyon Road. (Registered overnight guests at Zion Lodge can drive their own vehicles to the hotel.)

In Bryce, the shuttle bus is not required, but is highly recommended during peak season. The bus picks up visitors at the park gate and drives the length of the main parkway, stopping at all the major trailheads and viewpoints, in addition to campgrounds, Ruby's Inn, and the Lodge at Bryce Canyon. Using the shuttle is required in Bryce if your vehicle is 20 feet (6 m) or longer.

## TOURS

Bus tours of Utah's national parks, often in conjunction with Grand Canyon National Park, are available from several regional tour companies. **Southern Utah Scenic Tours** (435/656-1504 or 888/404-8687; http://utahscenictours.com) offers multiday scenic and thematic tours.

**Road Scholar** (800/454-5768; www.roadscholar.org) operates programs out of St. George, including a bus tour of southern Utah. These trips are geared toward older adults and involve some easy hiking.

For a truly unusual bus tour, consider the **Adventure Bus** (375 S. Main St., Moab; 909/633-7225 or 888/737-5263; www.adventurebus.com), a bus that's had most of its seats removed to make a lounge and sleeping areas. Guests live on the bus (some meals are provided) as it makes tours of Utah and other Southwest hot spots.

## STREET NUMBERING AND GRID ADDRESSES

Many towns founded by Latter-day Saint settlers share a street-numbering scheme that can be confusing to first-time visitors but quickly becomes intuitive. A city's address grid will generally have its temple at the center, with blocks numbered by hundreds out in every direction. For instance, 100 West is one block west of the center of town, then comes 200 West, and so on. In conversation, you may hear the shorthand "4th South," "3rd West," and so on to indicate 400 South or 300 West.

While this street-numbering system is a picture of precision, it's also confusing at first. All addresses have four parts: When you see the address 436 North 100 West, for instance, the system tells you that the address will be found four blocks north of the center of town, on 100 West. One rule of thumb is to remember that the last two segments of an address (300 South, 500 East, 2300 West) are the street's actual name—the equivalent of a single street signifier such as Oak Street or Front Avenue.

# NEARBY TOWNS
## NEAR ZION
### Springdale

With its location just outside Zion's south entrance, Springdale (pop. 650) is geared toward park visitors. Its many high-quality hotels and B&Bs, as well as frequent free shuttle bus service to the park's entrance, make Springdale an awesome base for a Zion trip.

#### FOOD

There are a number of food options in Springdale, including **Cafe Soleil** (205 Zion Park Blvd.; 435/772-0505; www.cafesoleilzionpark.com; 6:30am-4pm daily spring-fall, 8am-4pm winter; $8-12), a bright, friendly place for breakfast or a lunchtime sandwich that's a short walk from the park entrance. Springdale's sole brewpub is the **Zion Canyon Brew Pub** (95 Zion Park Blvd.; 435/772-0336; www.zionbrewery.com;

11:30am-10pm daily; $15-29), right at the pedestrian gate to the park.

**King's Landing Bistro** (1515 Zion Park Blvd.; 435/772-7422; www.klbzion.com; 5pm-9pm Tues.-Sat.; $23-35), located at the Driftwood Lodge, serves some of Springdale's most innovative dinners. The town's only full-fledged supermarket, **Sol Foods** (995 Zion Park Blvd.; 435/772-3100; www.solfoods.com; 7am-11pm daily), stocks groceries, deli items, hardware, and camping supplies.

## St. George

Southern Utah's largest city, St. George (pop. 93,000) sits between lazy bends of the Virgin River and rocky hills of red sandstone. With its strip malls, chain restaurants, and busy roads, the city itself won't appeal to most park travelers, but it makes a convenient stop en route to or from Zion. You'll find an abundance of hotels, a clutch of good restaurants, public art and galleries in the old downtown core, and lovely Snow Canyon State Park a few miles away.

## Cedar City

Cedar City (pop. about 33,000), known for its scenic setting and its summertime Utah Shakespeare Festival, is a handy base for exploring a good chunk of southern Utah. Zion National Park's Kolob Canyons area is less than 20 miles (32 km) from Cedar City. Within an easy day's drive are the Zion Canyon section of the park to the south and Bryce Canyon National Park.

# NEAR BRYCE

## Tropic

Tropic is 11 miles (17.7 km) east of Bryce Canyon National Park on Highway 12, and is visible from many of the park's viewpoints. Travelers think of Tropic primarily for its cache of motels lining Main Street (Hwy. 12), but you'll also find several pleasant B&Bs and great restaurants—as well as a back entrance into Bryce Amphitheater via Tropic Trail.

## Panguitch

Panguitch is one of the more pleasant towns in this part of Utah, with an abundance of reasonably priced motels,

downtown Springdale

plus a couple of good places to eat. It's a convenient stopover on the road between Zion and Bryce.

Panguitch is on U.S. 89, about 7 miles (11.3 km) north of Bryce Junction (Hwy. 12 and U.S. 89). From Bryce Junction, it is 11 miles (17.7 km) east on Highway 12 to Bryce Canyon National Park.

# RECREATION

Utah's national parks are home to red-rock canyons, towering arches, and needles of sandstone best explored by foot, bike, or boat. Hikers will find a variety of trails, ranging from paved accessible paths to remote backcountry hikes requiring advanced navigation. Rafts and jet boats out of Moab are another means to explore rugged canyons otherwise inaccessible to all but the hardiest trekkers. And sheer canyon walls and twisting towers offer incredible routes for experienced rock climbers—check park regulations before climbing, as restrictions or permitting may apply.

## HIKING

Utah's national parks offer lots of opportunities for hikers and backcountry enthusiasts interested in exploring the scenery on foot. Each of the parks has a variety of well-maintained hiking trails, ranging from easy strolls to multiday backcountry treks. In fact, the most compelling parts of Zion are accessible only by foot.

One popular activity is canyoneering, which involves navigating mazelike slot canyons. Hundreds of feet deep, but sometimes only wide enough for a hiker to squeeze through, these canyons are found across southern Utah. Many canyoneering routes require technical skills and equipment, including rappelling, scrambling, and wading or swimming. Flash floods also pose a major threat to canyoneers, so only go if the forecast is dry.

## CAMPING

All of Utah's national parks have campgrounds, and each park keeps at least one campground open year-round. Some campgrounds are first come, first served; reservations (877/444-6777; www.recreation.gov; reservation fee $8 online, $9 phone) are accepted seasonally at Zion's Watchman Campground and Bryce's Sunset Campground.

hiking in Bryce Canyon

During the summer and on holiday weekends in spring and fall, arrive at the park early in the day and select a campsite immediately. Don't expect to find hookups or showers at National Park Service campgrounds. For these comforts, look just outside the park entrance, where you'll generally find at least one full-service commercial campground.

## Backcountry Camping

Backcountry campers in national parks must stop by the park visitor center for a backcountry permit. Backcountry camping may be limited to specific sites in order to spread people out, in which case a park ranger will assign you a campground.

Before heading into the backcountry, check with a ranger about weather, water sources, fire danger, trail conditions, and regulations. Local gear stores and outfitters are also good sources of information. Here are some tips for traveling safely and respectfully in the backcountry:

- Tell rangers or other reliable people where you are going and when you expect to return; they'll alert rescuers if you go missing.

- Travel in small groups for the best experience (group size may also be regulated).

- Avoid stepping on—or camping on—fragile cryptobiotic soils.

- Use a portable stove to avoid leaving fire scars.

- Resist the temptation to shortcut switchbacks; this causes erosion and can be dangerous.

- Avoid digging tent trenches or cutting vegetation.

- Help preserve old Native American and other historic ruins.

- Camp at least 300 (91 m) away from springs, creeks, and trails. Camp at least 0.25 mile (0.4 km)

from a lone water source to avoid scaring away wildlife and livestock.

- Avoid camping in washes at any time; be alert to thunderstorms.

- Take care not to throw or kick rocks off trails—someone might be below you.

- Don't drink water directly from streams or lakes, no matter how clean the water appears; it may contain the parasitic protozoan *Giardia lamblia*, which causes giardiasis. Boiling water for several minutes will kill giardia as well as most other bacterial or viral pathogens. Chemical treatments and water filters usually work too, although they're not as reliable as boiling (giardia spends part of its life in a hard shell that protects it from most chemicals).

- Bathe and wash dishes away from lakes, streams, and springs. Use biodegradable soap, and scatter your wash water.

- Bring a trowel for personal sanitation. Dig 6-8 inches (15-20 cm) deep and cover your waste; in some areas, you'll be required to carry portable human waste disposal systems.

- Pack out all your trash, including toilet paper and feminine hygiene items.

- Bring plenty of feed for your horses and mules.

- Leave dogs at home; they're not permitted on national park trails.

- If you realize you're lost, find shelter. If you're sure of a way to civilization and plan to walk out, leave a note with your departure time and planned route.

# THE AMERICA THE BEAUTIFUL PASS

The U.S. government has revamped its park pass system, inaugurating a new set of annual passes that are the result of a cooperative effort between the National Park Service, the U.S. Forest Service, the U.S. Fish and Wildlife Service, the Bureau of Land Management, and the Bureau of Reclamation.

The **basic pass** is called the America the Beautiful—National Parks and Federal Recreational Lands Pass (valid for 1 year from date of purchase; $80 plus a $5 processing and handling fee), which is available to the general public and provides access to, and use of, federal recreation sites that charge an entrance or standard amenity fee. Passes can be obtained in person at a park; by calling 888/ASK-USGS—888/275-8747, ext. 1; or at http://store.usgs.gov/pass.

U.S. citizens or permanent residents ages 62 or older can purchase a **lifetime version** of the America the Beautiful pass for $80. This pass can only be obtained in person at a park. The Senior Pass provides free access to federal parks and recreational areas, plus a 50 percent discount on some fees, such as camping, swimming, boat launch, and specialized interpretive services.

Both passes are good for the cardholder plus three adults (ages 15 and under are free). The pass is nontransferable and generally does not cover or reduce special recreation permit fees or fees charged by park concessionaires.

U.S. citizens or permanent residents with permanent disabilities are eligible for a free lifetime **America the Beautiful Access Pass.** Documentation such as a statement from a licensed physician, the Veterans Administration, or Social Security is required to obtain this pass, which can only be obtained in person at a park. Like the Senior Pass, the Access Pass provides free access to federal parks and recreational areas, plus a 50 percent discount on some fees, such as camping, swimming, boat launch, and specialized interpretive services. Free annual passes are also available to members of the U.S. military and their families.

Volunteers who have amassed 250 service hours with one of the participating federal agencies are eligible for a **free one-year pass,** which is available through their supervisor.

---

- Visit the Leave No Trace website (www.lnt.org) for more details on responsible backcountry travel.

## CLIMBING

While there's no climbing found in Bryce, most visitors to Zion enjoy spotting rock climbers scaling canyon walls and sandstone pillars. Generally, climbing in Zion is not beginner-friendly—although there are a few boulder problems near the park's south entrance. Aside from requiring experience lead climbing with trad (traditional protection) on multi-pitch routes, sandstone poses its own set of challenges—it weakens when wet, so you can't climb after rain to avoid damaging the rock.

Climbers in Zion must observe clean climbing techniques. This includes sticking to established approach trails to prevent further erosion, using colored chalk to avoid leaving marks, carrying out all (including human) waste, and not leaving any new hardware behind, except to replace existing anchors or bolts.

Climbing season is spring or fall. During the summer, the walls become extremely hot. Some climbing areas may be closed during the spring to protect nesting raptors. Check at the visitor centers for current closures and to obtain permits; most parks require obtaining a free permit to climb.

## RANGER PROGRAMS
### ZION

Except for ranger-led walks, classes organized by Zion National Park Forever, horseback rides from Zion Lodge, and the running commentary from talkative shuttle-bus drivers, Zion is a do-it-yourself park. Outfitters are not permitted to lead trips within the park. If you'd like a guided tour outside park boundaries—where you'll find equally stunning scenery—several outfitters in Springdale lead cycling, canyoneering, and climbing trips.

The best way to get a feel for Zion's impressive geology and habitats is to participate in one of the ranger-led nature programs and hikes offered late March-November; check the posted schedule at the Zion Canyon Visitor Center. Children's programs, including the popular Junior Ranger program, are held intermittently in March-April and daily Memorial Day-mid-August at Zion Nature Center near South Campground; ask at the visitor center for details.

**Zion National Park Forever** (435/772-3264; www.zionpark.org) runs educational programs in the park, which include animal tracking, photography, and archaeology; fees vary.

### BRYCE

Rangers offer geology talks and rim walks throughout the year, as well as summer evening programs on park natural history and other topics. In summer,

when the conditions are right, rangers also offer Full Moon Hikes and "star parties" with telescopes trained on distant galaxies. In winter, when snowfall allows, rangers also lead beginner-oriented snowshoe hikes (snowshoes provided) that explore the park's winter ecology.

For schedules and more information, check out the listings on the park website (www.nps.gov/brca) or look at the list posted at the visitor center.

## ACCESSIBILITY

Travelers with disabilities will find Utah progressive when it comes to accessibility. Both Zion and Bryce Canyon National Parks have all-abilities trails and services. Both national parks have reasonably good facilities for visitors with limited mobility. Visitor centers are all accessible, and at least a couple of trails in each park are paved or smooth enough for wheelchair users to navigate with some assistance. Each park has a few accessible campsites.

Most hotels also offer some form of barrier-free lodging. It's best to call ahead and inquire what accommodations are available, however, because services can vary from one establishment to another.

## TRAVELING WITH PETS

Unless you really have no other option, it's best not to bring your dog (or cat, or bird, or ferret) along on a national park vacation. Although pets are allowed in national parks, they aren't permitted on the trails. This limits you and your dog to leashed walks along the roads, around campground loops, and in parking areas. During much of the year, it's far too hot to leave an animal in a parked car.

In Zion, private cars are prohibited on the scenic canyon drive during much of the year, and no pets are allowed on shuttle buses. The closest options for dog day care are over in Hurricane and

# DARK SKIES

starry skies in Zion National Park

Far from light pollution, Bryce Canyon National Park is recognized as an **International Dark Sky Park,** and the stars here really do pop out of the night sky. Astronomy buffs should visit in winter when skies are clearest, or in mid-June, when the park holds a four-day **Astronomy Festival,** with guest speakers, workshops, and constellation "tours."

More casual guided stargazing is possible several times a week during the summer when rangers lead **astronomy programs,** usually with a telescope at the visitor center. For the most brilliant views of the Milky Way, visit around the new moon, when skies are darkest. On the other hand, full-moon nights often bring a chance to take a ranger-led **moonlit hike.**

The real experts are found at **Dark Ranger Observatory** (1-mile South, East Fork Rd. 087, Bryce Canyon; 435/590-9498; darkrangertelescopetours. com; adults $42, kids $11; reservations required), just 10 minutes southeast of the park entrance. The Dark Rangers host nightly viewings May-October, as well three viewings a week during the off-season.

On your own, head out to **Yovimpa Point** to get a look at the Milky Way or view the Perseid meteor showers in mid-August. Bring a proper flashlight to make your way back to your car.

Although Zion's night sky is not as celebrated, a nighttime walk along the **Pa'rus Trail,** with the rock cliffs etched against the sky, is certainly beautiful. Even better views come from the **Kolob Terrace** or **Kolob Canyons** areas, both of which are outside Zion Canyon.

include On the Spot Play and Stay and Zion Canyon Recreation Center & Spa.

# HEALTH AND SAFETY

Take a few precautions to minimize the very reasonable risks that exist in Utah's parks. For the most part, using common sense about the dangers of extreme temperatures, remote backcountry exploration, and wildlife encounters will ensure a safe and healthy trip.

## HEAT AND WATER

Southern Utah in late spring, summer, and early fall is a very hot place. Use sunscreen and wear a wide-brimmed hat and good sunglasses with full UV protection. A sun shirt with built-in UPF protection is also a good idea. Heat exhaustion can be a problem if you're out in the hot sun. In midsummer, get an early start. If you're out during the heat of the afternoon, take breaks in the shade when the sun shines its brightest.

Always bring plenty of water and drink steadily throughout the day, whether you're thirsty or not, rather than gulping huge amounts of water once you feel thirsty. For hikers, one of the best ways to drink enough is to carry water in a hydration pack. One easy way to tell if you're getting enough to drink is to monitor your urine output. If you're only urinating a couple times a day, and the color and odor of your urine are strong, it's time to start drinking more.

## HYPOTHERMIA

Just because you're in the Utah desert, it doesn't mean you're immune to hypothermia. This lowering of the body's temperature below 95°F (35°C) causes disorientation, uncontrollable shivering, slurred speech, and drowsiness. The victim may not even realize what's wrong. Unless corrective action is taken immediately, hypothermia can lead to death. Hikers should therefore travel with companions and always carry wind and rain protection. Space blankets are lightweight and cheap and offer protection against the cold in emergencies.

Remember that temperatures can plummet rapidly in Utah's dry climate—a drop of 40 degrees Fahrenheit (22 degrees C) between day and night is common. Be especially careful at high elevations, where sunshine can quickly change into freezing rain or a blizzard. Simply falling into a mountain stream can also lead to hypothermia and death unless proper action is taken. If you're cold and tired, don't waste time: Seek shelter and build a fire, change into dry clothes, and drink warm liquids. If a victim isn't fully conscious, warm them up with skin-to-skin contact in a sleeping bag. Try to keep the victim awake and offer plenty of warm liquids.

## GIARDIA

*Giardia lamblia* is a protozoan that has become common in even the most remote mountain streams. It is carried in animal or human waste that is deposited or washed into the water. When ingested, it begins reproducing, causing intense cramping and diarrhea in the host—this can become serious and may require medical attention.

No matter how clear a stream looks, it's best to assume that it is contaminated and to take precautions against giardia by filtering, boiling, or treating water with chemicals before drinking it. A high-quality filter will remove giardia and a host of other things you don't want to be drinking. (Spend a bit extra for one that removes particles down to one micrometer in size.) It's also effective to simply boil your water. Two to five minutes at a rolling boil will kill giardia even in the cyst stage. Because water boils at a lower temperature as elevation increases, increase the boiling time to 15 minutes if you're at 9,000 feet (2,743 m) or higher. Two drops of bleach left in a quart of water for 30 minutes will remove most giardia, although some microorganisms are resistant to chemicals.

## CORONAVIRUS

As Utah's Department of Health monitors COVID-19 cases and transmission through the state, phased guidelines requiring masks or social distance may change locally, so check the websites below regularly. Outside national parks, in small-town Utah, you'll find that people are less likely to wear masks than in major U.S. cities, even if a mandate is in place.

Moon encourages its readers to be courteous and ethical in their travel. We ask travelers to be respectful to residents, and mindful of the evolving situation in their chosen destination when planning their trip.

### Resources

Monitor the following websites to keep track of the evolving COVID-19 situation in Utah.

- **Utah Health Department:** https://coronavirus.utah.gov
- **Utah State Travel Bureau:** www.visitutah.com/ plan-your-trip/covid-19
- **National Park Service:** www. nps.gov/planyourvisit/alerts.htm

## HANTAVIRUS

Hantavirus is an infectious disease agent first isolated during the Korean War, then discovered in the Americas in 1993 by scientists in New Mexico. It occurs naturally throughout most of the Americas, especially in desert conditions. The infectious agent is airborne, and in the absence of prompt medical attention, its infections are usually fatal. Hantavirus pulmonary syndrome (HPS) can affect anyone, but with some fundamental knowledge, it's also easily prevented.

The natural host of the hantavirus appears to be rodents, especially mice and rats. The virus is not usually transmitted directly from rodents to humans. Rather, the rodents shed hantavirus particles in their saliva, urine, and droppings. Humans usually contract HPS by inhaling particles infected with the hantavirus. The virus becomes airborne when the particles dry out and

get stirred into the air (especially from sweeping a floor or shaking a rug). Humans then inhale these particles, which leads to infection.

HPS is not considered a highly infectious disease, so people usually contract HPS from long-term exposure. Because transmission usually occurs through inhalation, it's easiest for a human being to contract hantavirus within a contained environment, where the virus-infected particles aren't thoroughly dispersed. Being in a cabin or barn where rodents are found poses elevated risks for contracting the infection.

Simply traveling to a place where the hantavirus is known to occur is not considered a risk factor. Camping, hiking, and other outdoor activities also pose low risk, especially if steps are taken to reduce rodent contact. If you happen to stay in a rodent-infested cabin, thoroughly wet any droppings and dead rodents with a chlorine bleach solution (one cup of bleach per gallon of water) and let them stand for a few minutes before cleaning up. Wear rubber gloves and double-bag your garbage.

The first symptoms of HPS can occur anywhere between five days and three weeks after infection. They almost always include fever, fatigue, aching muscles (usually in the back, shoulders, or thighs), and other flu-like symptoms. Other early symptoms may include headaches, dizziness, chills, and abdominal discomfort such as vomiting, nausea, or diarrhea. These symptoms are shortly followed by intense coughing and shortness of breath. If you have these symptoms, seek medical help immediately. Untreated infections of hantavirus are almost always fatal.

## THUNDERSTORMS AND FLASH FLOODS

While southern Utah is a desert with little rainfall, summer is monsoon season, which usually kicks off around July 4 and runs through much of September. Thunderstorms can bring hazards to recreationalists in the area in the form of lightning strikes on exposed trails, dirt roads that become muddy and thus impassable, and, most notably, flash floods.

For those traveling through canyons—whether on a casual hike, by raft, by car, or via a canyoneering adventure—flash floods pose a major hazard that can lead to serious injury or death. Water rises rapidly, and violently rushes down narrow canyons, carrying debris with it. Before entering a canyon or heading down a dirt road, check the forecast and the skies. Visitor centers across the area are a great resource to evaluate the weather against your plans. Throughout your adventure, keep a tab on the skies and turn back if threatening storm clouds begin to form.

## THINGS THAT BITE OR STING

There are a few critters to watch out for in southern Utah, including snakes, scorpions, and spiders.

### Snakes

Rattlesnakes are present throughout southern Utah. Even though their venom is toxic, full venom injections are relatively uncommon, and, like all rattlesnakes, they pose little threat unless they're provoked.

If you see a rattlesnake, observe it at a safe distance. Be careful where you put your hands when canyoneering or scrambling—it's not a good idea to reach above your head and blindly plant your hands on a sunny rock ledge. Hikers should wear sturdy boots to minimize the chance that a snake's fangs will reach the skin if a bite occurs. Do not walk barefoot outside after dark—this is when snakes hunt.

Most people who receive medical treatment after being bitten by a rattlesnake live to tell the story. Prompt administration of antivenin is the most important treatment, and the most important aspect of first aid is to arrange transportation of the victim to a hospital as quickly as possible.

### Scorpions

A scorpion's sting isn't as painful as you'd expect (it's like a bee sting), and the venom is insufficient to cause any real harm. Still, it's not what you'd call pleasant, and experienced desert campers know to shake out their boots every morning, as scorpions and spiders are attracted to warm, moist, dark places. Occasionally, a scorpion sting can cause more severe temporary reactions.

### Spiders

Tarantulas and black widow spiders are present across much of the Colorado Plateau. Believe it or not, a tarantula's bite does not poison humans. The enzymes secreted when they bite turn the insides of frogs, lizards, and insects to a soft mush, allowing the tarantula to suck the guts from its prey. Another interesting tarantula fact: While males live about as long as you'd expect a spider to live, female tarantulas can live for up to 25 years. Females do sometimes eat the males, which may account for some of this disparity in longevity.

Black widow spiders, on the other hand, have a toxic bite. Although the bite is usually painless, it delivers a potent neurotoxin, which quickly causes pain, nausea, and vomiting. It is important to seek immediate treatment for a black widow bite. Although few people actually die from these bites, recovery is helped along considerably by antivenin.

## RESOURCES

**The American Southwest**
**www.americansouthwest.net/utah**
This online Utah guide provides an overview of national parks, national recreation areas, and some state parks.

**Desert USA**
**www.desertusa.com**
Desert USA's Utah section discusses places to visit and what plants and animals you might meet there. Here's the best part of this site: You can find out what's in bloom at www.desertusa.com/wildflo/nv.html.

### National Park Service
**www.nps.gov**
At this site, the National Park Service offers information for every park. You can also enter this address followed by a slash and the first two letters of the first two words of the place (first four letters if there's just a one-word name); for example, www.nps.gov/brca takes you to Bryce Canyon National Park and www.nps.gov/zion leads to Zion National Park.

### Recreation.gov
**www.recreation.gov**
If a campground is operated by the federal government, this is the place to make a reservation. You can expect to pay close to $9 for this convenience.

### Reserve America
**www.reserveamerica.com**
Use this website to reserve campsites in state campgrounds. It costs a few extra bucks to reserve a campsite, but compare that with the cost of being skunked out of a site and having to resort to a motel room.

### Greater Zion
**www.utahsdixie.com**
Utah's southwestern city of St. George is the focus of this site, which also covers some of the smaller communities outside Zion National Park.

### Utah Travel Council
**https://utah.com**
The Utah Travel Council is a one-stop shop for all sorts of information on Utah. It takes you around the state to sights, activities, events, and maps, and offers links to local tourism offices. The accommodations listings are the most up-to-date source for current room rates and options.

### Zion Park
**www.zionpark.com**
This site will point you to information on Springdale and the area surrounding Zion National Park, with links to lodging and restaurant sites.

### Zion National Park Forever
**www.zionpark.org**
Learn about (and purchase tickets for) upcoming educational programs in Zion National Park.

### Ruby's Inn
**www.rubysinn.com**
Book activities in Bryce Canyon National Park, from ATV tours to horseback rides.

### Canyoneering USA
**www.canyoneeringusa.com**
Created and maintained by a canyoneering enthusiast who's also the maker of gear for the sport, Tom's Utah Canyoneering Guide offers detailed beta on routes throughout southern Utah, including in Zion.

# INDEX

# LIST OF MAPS

# PHOTO CREDITS

All photos © Maya Silver except page 1 © Galyna Andrushko | Dreamstime.com; page 7 © Robert Bohrer | Dreamstime.com; page 9 © Hpbfotos | Dreamstime.com; page 10 © Jason P Ross | Dreamstime.com; Brianwelker | Dreamstime.com; page 11 © Hpbfotos | Dreamstime.com; page 12 © Osmar01 | Dreamstime.com; page 13 © Jocrebbin | Dreamstime.com; page 14 © Demerzel21 | Dreamstime.com; page 15 © Kobuspeche | Dreamstime.com; Sardonical | Dreamstime.com; page 16 © Chon Kit Leong | Dreamstime.com; page 18 © Humorousking207 | Dreamstime.com; page 19 © David Crane | Dreamstime.com; page 21 © Harris Shiffman | Dreamstime.com; page 23 © Zhukovsky | Dreamstime.com; Frank Bach | Dreamstime.com; page 28 © Frank Bach | Dreamstime.com; page 30 © Nicola Pulham | Dreamstime.com; page 32 © Bill McRae; page 33 © Cheri Alguire | Dreamstime.com; page 34 © Photosbyjam | Dreamstime.com; page 35 © Karen Foley | Dreamstime.com; page 37 © Oren Gelbendorf | Dreamstime.com; page 40 © Evdoha | Dreamstime.com; page 41 © Kenneth Keifer | Dreamstime.com; Cosbygerald | Dreamstime.com; Larry Gevert | Dreamstime.com; page 43 © Jimfeliciano | Dreamstime.com; page 47 © Judy Jewell; Coleong | Dreamstime.com; page 48 © Empro1 | Dreamstime.com; page 51 © Rpulham | Dreamstime.com; page 52 © Peter.wey | Dreamstime.com; Raphoto | Dreamstime.com; Osmar01 | Dreamstime.com; page 53 © William Perry | Dreamstime.com; page 54 © Skiserge1 | Dreamstime.com; page 55 © Raphoto | Dreamstime.com; Bbeckphoto | Dreamstime.com; page 56 © Fernley | Dreamstime.com; page 57 © Bill McRae; page 63 © Moehlestephen | Dreamstime.com; page 64 © Raphoto | Dreamstime.com; Gene Zhang | Dreamstime.com; Mikhail Dudarev | Dreamstime.com; page 66 © Peteleclerc | Dreamstime.com; page 67 © Swtrekker | Dreamstime.com; page 68 © CheriAlguire | Dreamstime.com; page 69 © Jennyt | Dreamstime.com; page 70 © Brian Wolski | Dreamstime.com; page 73 © ScenincMedia | Dreamstime.com; page 80 © Demerzel21 | Dreamstime.com; page 81 © Hpbfotos | Dreamstime.com; Claffra | Dreamstime.com; page 82 © Ryancheneyart | Dreamstime.com; page 83 © NPS / J. Cowley; Cgardinerphotos | Dreamstime.com; page 87 © Bill McRae; page 88 © Demerzel21 | Dreamstime.com; page 89 © Lightphoto | Dreamstime.com; page 90 © Jaahnlieb | Dreamstime.com; Sainaniritu | Dreamstime.com; page 91 © Mandj98 | Dreamstime.com; Revoc9 | Dreamstime.com; Bill McRae; page 92 © William Perry | Dreamstime.com; page 94 © Humorousking207 | Dreamstime.com; Gnagel | Dreamstime.com; Judy Jewell; page 95 © Jeremyarnica | Dreamstime.com; page 101 © Emmajay1 | Dreamstime.com; page 104 © Hellen8 | Dreamstime.com; Kelly Vandellen | Dreamstime.com; page 109 © Donyanedomam | Dreamstime.com; page 114 © Jaahnlieb | Dreamstime.com; Bpperry | Dreamstime.com; page 115 © Stefano Caccia | Dreamstime.com; page 116 © Stephen Moehle | Dreamstime.com; page 119 © Bpperry | Dreamstime.com; page 121 © Evan Spiler | Dreamstime.com; page 123 © David Crane | Dreamstime.com; page 126 © Melani Wright | Dreamstime.com; Christopher Bellette | Dreamstime.com; page 127 © Melani Wright | Dreamstime.com; page 128 © Jaahnlieb | Dreamstime.com; page 129 © Melani Wright | Dreamstime.com; page 130 © Donald Roy | Dreamstime.com; page 131 © Carrie Davis | Dreamstime.com; page 133 © Kan1234 | Dreamstime.com; page 139 © Brandi Smalls; page 143 © Adogslifephoto | Dreamstime.com

# National Parks Travel Guides from Moon

**MOON**
## ACADIA
### NATIONAL PARK
SEASIDE TOWNS · FALL FOLIAGE
CYCLING & PADDLING

HILARY NANGLE

**MOON**
## ARCHES &
## CANYONLANDS
### NATIONAL PARKS
HIKING · BIKING
SCENIC DRIVES

JUDY JEWELL & W. C. MCRAE

**MOON**
## BANFF
### NATIONAL PARK
HIKE · CAMP
SEE WILDLIFE

ANDREW HEMPSTEAD

**MOON**
## CANADIAN
## ROCKIES
WITH BANFF & JASPER NATIONAL PARKS
SCENIC DRIVES · WILDLIFE
HIKING & SKIING

ANDREW HEMPSTEAD

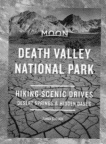

**MOON**
## DEATH VALLEY
## NATIONAL PARK
HIKING · SCENIC DRIVES
DESERT SPRINGS & HIDDEN OASES

LARA DUNSTON

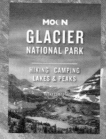

**MOON**
## GLACIER
### NATIONAL PARK
HIKING · CAMPING
LAKES & PEAKS

BECKY LOMAX

**MOON**
## GRAND
## CANYON
HIKE · CAMP
RAFT THE
COLORADO RIVER

TIM HULL

**MOON**
## GREAT SMOKY
## MOUNTAINS
### NATIONAL PARK
HIKING · CAMPING
SCENIC DRIVES

JASON FRYE

**MOON**
## JOSHUA TREE
## & PALM SPRINGS
HIKING · SCENIC DRIVES
DESERT GETAWAYS

JENNA BLOUGH

**MOON**
## ROCKY
## MOUNTAIN
### NATIONAL PARK
HIKE · CAMP
SEE WILDLIFE

ERIN ENGLISH

**MOON**
## SEQUOIA &
## KINGS CANYON
HIKING · CAMPING
WATERFALLS & BIG TREES

LEIGH BENNACHE

**MOON**
## YELLOWSTONE
## & GRAND TETON
HIKE · CAMP
SEE WILDLIFE

**MOON**
## YOSEMITE
## SEQUOIA &
## KINGS CANYON
HIKING · CAMPING
WATERFALLS & BIG TREES

ANN MARIE BROWN

**MOON**
## ZION &
## BRYCE
WITH ARCHES, CANYONLANDS, CAPITOL REEF,
GRAND STAIRCASE-ESCALANTE & MORE
HIKING & BIKING
STARGAZING · SCENIC DRIVES

DANA DELVEY

# USA NATIONAL PARKS

THE COMPLETE GUIDE TO ALL

## 63 PARKS

BECKY LOMAX

Get the bestselling all-parks guide, or check out Moon's new Best Of Parks series to make the most of a 1-3 day visit to top parks.

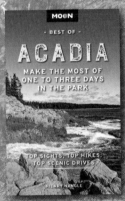

- BEST OF -

## ACADIA

MAKE THE MOST OF ONE TO THREE DAYS IN THE PARK

TOP SIGHTS, TOP HIKES, TOP SCENIC DRIVES

HILARY NANGLE

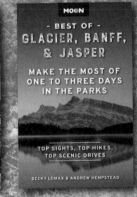

- BEST OF -

## GLACIER, BANFF, & JASPER

MAKE THE MOST OF ONE TO THREE DAYS IN THE PARKS

TOP SIGHTS, TOP HIKES, TOP SCENIC DRIVES

BECKY LOMAX & ANDREW HEMPSTEAD

- BEST OF -

## GRAND CANYON

MAKE THE MOST OF ONE TO THREE DAYS IN THE PARK

TOP SIGHTS, TOP HIKES, TOP SCENIC DRIVES

TIM HULL

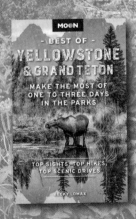

- BEST OF -

## YELLOWSTONE & GRAND TETON

MAKE THE MOST OF ONE TO THREE DAYS IN THE PARKS

TOP SIGHTS, TOP HIKES, TOP SCENIC DRIVES

BECKY LOMAX

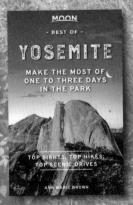

- BEST OF -

## YOSEMITE

MAKE THE MOST OF ONE TO THREE DAYS IN THE PARK

TOP SIGHTS, TOP HIKES, TOP SCENIC DRIVES

ANN MARIE BROWN

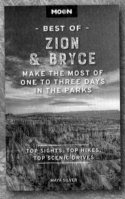

- BEST OF -

## ZION & BRYCE

MAKE THE MOST OF ONE TO THREE DAYS IN THE PARKS

TOP SIGHTS, TOP HIKES, TOP SCENIC DRIVES

MAYA SILVER

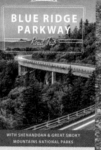

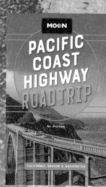

# ROAD TRIP GUIDES FROM MOON

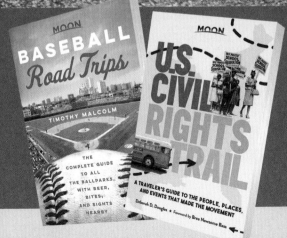

Explore the U.S. with expert authors like baseball writer Timothy Malcolm and journalist Deborah D. Douglas!

# Explore Near and Far with Moon Travel Guides

**MOON**

**Alaska**

Lisa Maloney

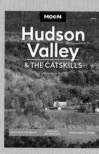

**MOON**

**Hudson Valley**

& THE CATSKILLS

Nikki Goth Itoi

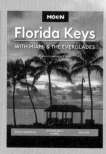

**MOON**

**Florida Keys**

WITH MIAMI & THE EVERGLADES

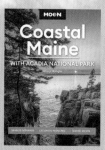

**MOON**

**Coastal Maine**

WITH ACADIA NATIONAL PARK

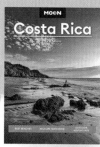

**MOON**

**Costa Rica**

**MOON**

**Greek Islands**

& ATHENS

**MOON**

**Japan**

**MOON**

**Maui**

Greg Archer

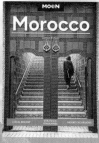

**MOON**

**Morocco**

**MOON**

**Puerto Rico**

**MOON**

**Idaho**

**MOON**

**Portugal**

WITH MADEIRA & THE AZORES

**MOON**

**Victoria**

& VANCOUVER ISLAND

Andrew Hempstead

**MOON**

**Scotland**

**MOON**

**Tahiti**

& FRENCH POLYNESIA

**MOON**

**Colorado**

# MAP SYMBOLS

| | | | | | | | |
|---|---|---|---|---|---|---|---|
| ═══ | Highway | ○ | City/Town | 🅿 | Parking Area | 🛆 | Small Park |
| ═══ | Primary Road | ◉ | State Capital | 🅃 | Trailhead | ▲ | Mountain Peak |
| ═══ | Secondary Road | ◈ | National Capital | 🅱 | Bike Trailhead | ✛ | Unique Natural Feature |
| ═ ═ ═ | Unpaved Road | ★ | Top 3 Sight | 🅐 | Camping | | |
| ---- | Trail | 🅺 | Top Hike | 🄰 | Picnic Area | ✦ | Unique Hydro Feature |
| ━━━ | Paved Trail | ★ | Highlight/Sight | Ⓜ | Mass Transit | 🝆 | Waterfall |
| ░░░ | Pedestrian Walkway | • | Accommodation | ✈ | Airport | ⛷ | Ski Area |
| ⋯⋯ | Ferry | ▼ | Restaurant/Bar | ✕ | Airfield | | |
| ━ ━ ━ | Railroad | ▪ | Other Site | ▲ | Place of Worship | ⬭ | Glacier |

# CONVERSION TABLES

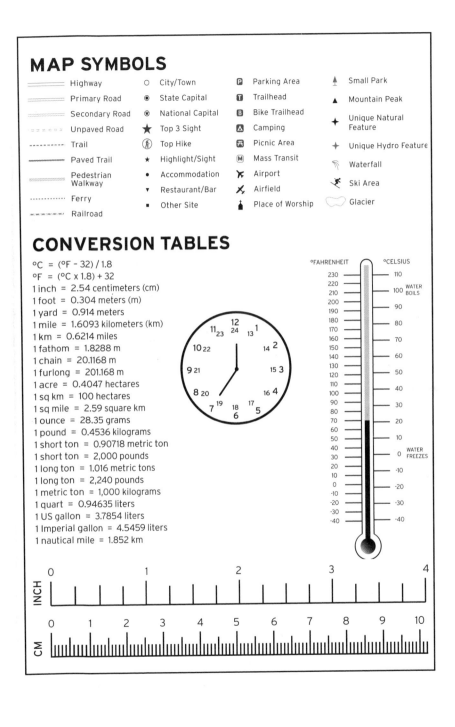

°C = (°F - 32) / 1.8
°F = (°C x 1.8) + 32
1 inch = 2.54 centimeters (cm)
1 foot = 0.304 meters (m)
1 yard = 0.914 meters
1 mile = 1.6093 kilometers (km)
1 km = 0.6214 miles
1 fathom = 1.8288 m
1 chain = 20.1168 m
1 furlong = 201.168 m
1 acre = 0.4047 hectares
1 sq km = 100 hectares
1 sq mile = 2.59 square km
1 ounce = 28.35 grams
1 pound = 0.4536 kilograms
1 short ton = 0.90718 metric ton
1 short ton = 2,000 pounds
1 long ton = 1.016 metric tons
1 long ton = 2,240 pounds
1 metric ton = 1,000 kilograms
1 quart = 0.94635 liters
1 US gallon = 3.7854 liters
1 Imperial gallon = 4.5459 liters
1 nautical mile = 1.852 km

**MOON BEST OF ZION & BRYCE**
Avalon Travel
Hachette Book Group
1700 Fourth Street
Berkeley, CA 94710, USA
www.moon.com

Editor: Vy Tran
Managing Editor: Courtney Packard
Copy Editor: Christopher Church
Graphics Coordinator: Darren Alessi
Production Coordinator: Darren Alessi
Cover Design: Marcie Lawrence
Interior Design: Tabitha Lahr
Map Editor: John Culp
Cartographer: John Culp
Proofreader: Jessica Gould
Indexer: Rachel Lyon

ISBN-13: 979-8-88647-032-1

Printing History
1st Edition — 2021
2nd Edition — February 2024
5 4 3 2 1

Text © 2024 by Maya Silver.
Maps © 2024 by Avalon Travel.
Some photos and illustrations are
used by permission and are the
property of the original copyright
owners.

Front cover photo: Bryce Canyon
National Park from Sunset Point ©
Jon Arnold Images Ltd / Alamy Stock
Photo
Back cover photos: The Narrows
© Stephen Moehle | Dreamstime.
com (top); hikers in Bryce Canyon ©
Agap13 | Dreamstime.com (middle);
ponderosa pine © Dean Pennala |
Dreamstime.com (bottom)
Back Flap photo: Fairyland Trail ©
Gene Zhang | Dreamstime.com

Printed in China by RRD APS